"Luke Powery's book *Becoming Human* is deeply testimonial, demonstrating how personal experiences are profoundly affected by the political and historical legacy of slavery and racism. Powery makes an original contribution by making connections between race issues and the theology of the Holy Spirit and homiletics. He makes a convincing case that racialization deprives humanity of the possibility of being human together, an approach to human life he views as a theological imperative and a spiritual discipline. This is an inspiring read and highly recommended!"

 —HYERAN KIM-CRAGG, **Principal and Timothy Eaton**
 Memorial Church Professor of Preaching, Emmanuel College
 of Victoria University in the University of Toronto

"In this timely and essential book, Luke Powery boldly unmasks the dehumanizing reality of colonial racialization (including in the church and its practices) and envisions a turn to humanization in the power of the Spirit. Drawing on historical analysis, personal experience, and the story of Pentecost, Powery shows how the Spirit can move the church beyond the oppressive hierarchies and divisions of racism toward the celebration of a diverse and inclusive humanity. He also suggests concrete ways that preaching and ministry can enflesh this revolutionary Pentecostal fire. Powery's impassioned 'Spirit speech' should be embraced by every pastor, seminary student, and congregation member."

 —CHARLES L. CAMPBELL, **James T. and Alice Mead Cleland**
 Professor Emeritus of Homiletics, Duke Divinity School

"In this age of division and factionalism, many have forgotten what it is to become human. There might not be any book that is more appropriate for this and every time for those who desire that our nation, church, and world be more humane."

 —FRANK A. THOMAS, **Director of the PhD Program**
 in African American Preaching and Sacred Rhetoric,
 Christian Theological Seminary

"Pentecost is pedagogy for the human race. This is the grounding thesis of Luke Powery's revolutionary work *Becoming Human*. Powery deconstructs nonsensical notions of color blindness and asks the church universal to reclaim her birthright and become her intended self—a multiethnic, multilingual, mosaic polyphony of holy fire and breath, bodies, and tongues, all proclaiming God—while naming as sin the dehumanizing effects of racialization and cultural erasure. Turning toward the Spirit, Powery makes clear, implies a turning toward an incarnational God who sees difference differently and invites human beings to embrace their creatureliness as a gift of the Spirit.

Homiletics and cultural studies scholars will find here an academically robust, first-rate discussion on preaching and race, and religious practitioners will no doubt recognize that the wind of the Spirit has breathed on Powery's pen."

—KENYATTA R. GILBERT, Professor of Homiletics,
Howard University School of Divinity

"Many titles, images, and roles exist for the Holy Spirit; Luke Powery lifts up another: the Spirit as humanizer. In this book, Powery suggests that the Spirit is the one who humanizes us in the face of one of the most destructively dehumanizing forces our society has known: racism. This 'pneumatology of race' is timely as the church and world are in need of having their racialized imaginations 'troubled.' For those who struggle to develop an ecclesial theological response to racism, Powery says, let us look to the Spirit of Pentecost for what we preach and how we practice the faith. A pneumatological response to racism is unfortunately rare to find in the theological academy, yet Powery's meditation demonstrates both its fittingness and urgency. This work resounds with sobering conviction and expectant hope."

—DANIEL CASTELO, William Kellon Quick Professor of
Theology and Methodist Studies and Director of the Center
for Studies in the Wesleyan Tradition, Duke University
Divinity School

"Luke Powery redefines what it means to preach in the power of the Spirit. This exciting volume lays out a vibrant pneumatology and pairs it with an illuminating analysis of Howard Thurman's best teaching on the spiritual life. Ultimately, Powery's prophetic vision upends the racist frameworks that hinder the church's embrace of humanity and shows us how to dance with the Spirit. In a word: dynamic."

—DONYELLE C. McCRAY, Associate Professor of Homiletics,
Yale Divinity School

"Two thousand years ago there were Arab, Cretan, and Roman (among other) tongues spoken on the streets of Jerusalem. It took a physician known as Luke to record these voices as declaring the wondrous and powerful works of God. In our fraught 2020s, we can thank another doctor (of divinity), Luke Powery, for translating the witnesses of (especially but not only) Black communities to all of us (including especially but not only white readers) so that we can appreciate how these experiences testify to and declare the prophetic words of God for our time."

—AMOS YONG, Professor of Theology in Mission and
Dean of the School of Mission and Theology, Fuller Seminary

Becoming Human

Carol,

may the Spirit blow
at you as you read.
You are a gift
of the Spirit and
a gift to the
Duke community.
Peace + Blessings,

[signature]

11/27/22

Becoming Human

The Holy Spirit and the Rhetoric of Race

Luke A. Powery

WESTMINSTER
JOHN KNOX PRESS
LOUISVILLE · KENTUCKY

First edition
Published by Westminster John Knox Press
Louisville, Kentucky

22 23 24 25 26 27 28 29 30 31—10 9 8 7 6 5 4 3 2 1

Book design by Drew Stevens
Cover design by Lisa Buckley Design

Library of Congress Cataloging-in-Publication Data
Names: Powery, Luke A., 1974- author.
Title: Becoming human : the Holy Spirit and the rhetoric of race / Luke A. Powery.
Description: First edition. | Louisville, Kentucky : Westminster John Knox Press, [2022] | Includes index. | Summary: "Urges the church to live up to the inclusive story of Pentecost in its worship life"-- Provided by publisher.
Identifiers: LCCN 2022030090 (print) | LCCN 2022030091 (ebook) | ISBN 9780664267223 (paperback) | ISBN 9781646982875 (ebook)
Subjects: LCSH: Holy Spirit. | Theological anthropology--Christianity.
Classification: LCC BT121.3 P69 2022 (print) | LCC BT121.3 (ebook) | DDC 231/.3--dc23/eng/20220808
LC record available at https://lccn.loc.gov/2022030090
LC ebook record available at https://lccn.loc.gov/2022030091

Most Westminster John Knox Press books are available at special quantity discounts when purchased in bulk by corporations, organizations, and special-interest groups. For more information, please e-mail SpecialSales@wjkbooks.com.

For the Rev. Dr. William C. Turner Jr.,
a human gift of the Spirit

Contents

Foreword

"Where can I go from Your spirit, and where from before You flee?" So says the psalmist in Psalm 139, indicating an eternal truth: not simply that the Spirit of the living God is everywhere, but that the Spirit is inescapable. The scholastic designation that God is omnipresent is much too sterile a design to capture what is at stake in this declaration. God travels the journey with each individual creature. God is there at the beginning of the journey, God is in the journey's middle, and God meets us where we arrive. God meets us where we run, where we hide, and where we believe we are hidden beyond sight. Divine presence is therefore not a noun but a verb—the constant being here and there with us. But the psalmist's question must be placed alongside another question, more urgent and poignant: why do we resist the Spirit of the living God?

The fact that we resist the Spirit of the living God is the fundamental conundrum of human existence. That fact sits between the mystery of sin and the mystery of a God who cannot be thwarted in God's willingness to be thwarted. We could speak of this as the thorns of human freedom that God feels, even as Jesus had them pressed down on his head. But the question of resistance is not a matter of the complexities of God's providence. Our resisting God points to the stubbornness in our hearts, even as we stare into the face of God. We meet that face in Jesus Christ and then, through the light cast by his face, we see God's image in the faces of other human creatures. It is precisely that image in the faces of other human creatures and our resistance to it that concern Luke Powery.

Powery is bringing together these two questions—where can we hide from the Spirit of God, and how is it that we can resist the Spirit of God?—at the site of race and the racial condition of the Western world. The racial condition of the Western world points to a resistance to the Spirit of God, a resistance that has come to be canonized. In one way we could discern that resistance as ancient, even primordial. But in another it is new in the sense of being launched at a particular moment, the colonial moment from the fifteenth century forward, and from a particular region of this planet, which will come to be called Europe by people who will eventually map an entire planet from their particular geographic, philosophical, and theological perspective.

Yet that resistance is also new in the sense of its ongoing generation, each day and each minute that people grasp more tightly the racial logics that continue to dominate the lives of so many. Where we lodge its beginning is less important than from where we see it and how we experience it. Powery examines that resistance from the position of the pulpit, from the work of the pastor, and from the lifeworld of a preacher.

Only from the embodied irony of being a preacher may one feel the thorns of this fundamental contradiction: Christians sometimes resisting the Spirit by refusing to see the full humanity of Black people and sometimes resisting the Spirit by resting comfortably in racial logics that nurture segregation, hierarchy, and white supremacy. A common theological mistake avoids considering our resistance to the Spirit of God by quickly and sloppily universalizing that resistance under the important theological rubric of sin and the sinful condition. Resistance is indeed sin, but its particularities are what matter not only to God but also to how we perceive divine presence working with us even in our resistance. The preaching life shows us that working and that resistance in slow motion, capturing its details inside the dual exegesis of texts and lives.

The Spirit of the living God flows through both—texts and lives—offering an interpretive and somatic intervention that might turn us not only toward the depth of our shared humanity, but also toward our new humanity in Christ. The Spirit can move through us and move us toward the new, if we are willing to yield. This is what Luke Powery is convinced of in this text; he has staked his argument on this pneumatological conviction.

Some would argue that at this moment in history this is a fool's errand. For many people, the racial antagonism of the Western world, the antiblackness embedded in Western institutional life and institutionalizing activities, the ease with which violence is perpetuated against Black flesh, and the lack of white mourning for that violence, do not point to resistance, even impenetrable resistance, but to the failure of a Christian God and of a faith formed in that God's name. For some people, resistance means a renunciation or a rejection of it all.

It takes faith to see resistance. This is what the experience of the

Spirit teaches us. Powery is drawing deeply on that pneumatological pedagogy because he understands what every serious preacher and every teacher of preachers knows: yielding to the Spirit of God is dangerous and sometimes frightening work. To yield is to reach into the depths of one's own humanity in recognition that God sees through every stratagem of concealment, every lie we tell ourselves, every denial and deceit that we believe protects our reputation, as well as the fears and wounds that hold us back from full living.

To yield to the Spirit of the living God is to live always on the edge of surprise, dangling in the holy wind, knowing that our life is not our own: we belong soul and body to God. Yet preaching must aim to move from the yielding of the one to the yielding of the many, from one preaching the word to many living the word, from asking, "Who will believe our report?" to seeing belief in action, embodied in the quotidian realities of Christians. This is the bridge—long and narrow, suspended over the rapid racial currents of our times—that must be crossed.

The first task is to get Christians to take seriously the Holy Spirit. It is well over one hundred years since the atomic bomb of the Azusa Street Mission, and we have seen decades of charismatic renewal permeating churches Catholic and Protestant, rich and poor, high and low, white and nonwhite. But in many church communities we have yet to see a yielding that shows the belief that the Spirit of God is flowing in and through us, thereby answering definitively the first question we asked; we cannot hide, nor do we wish to hide, from the Spirit of God.

Such embodied belief would mean rejecting the spells, incantations, and alchemies of our modern racecraft, and moving from acknowledging the humanity of Black folks to a full-throated advocacy for justice and thriving life for them and with them. Living into our confession of the full divinity of the Spirit is the unfinished business of Christian theology and life in the Western world, especially the global North. This is due in large measure to the idolatrous worship of the image of the white self-sufficient man that constantly subverts such Spirit-filled living.

The worship of that man holds out for many the hope of being like God, what Dietrich Bonhoeffer termed *sicut deus* life, life that aims to image God without listening to God, without acknowledging God, and certainly without communion with God and with our neighbors, both human and more than human. The formation of a healthy pneumatological vision of life continues to be thwarted, because we yet live in the age of that man where we are told to envision the Spirit through very limited options. The Spirit is either a hidden energy in us, vivifying our own designs and efforts, or the Spirit is a liturgical lapdog who comes when called, enlivening our worship, and turning Spirit-filled life into spectacle. This white self-sufficient man greets us daily with its inexhaustible stubbornness to accept the invitation to yield to the Spirit of the living God. How do we overcome that racialized stubbornness? Luke Powery would bring us back to the rough ground, back to Pentecost and the new humanity inaugurated there.

In fact, the first people Powery brings back to this rough ground are preachers caught in the racial now, tussling with a Christianity yet submerged in the historical trajectory of the racial imaginary with its intertwining of racism, capitalism, misogyny, and planetary exploitation. Preaching is difficult, and no preaching today—with the possible exception of preaching about sexuality—is more difficult or more demanding than preaching at the intersection of faith and race.

The tragedy at this moment is not only that ministers are refusing to preach about race (or sex), but also that when they do, they very often say absolutely nothing; that is, they say absolutely nothing that has to do with the new humanity established by the Holy Spirit. This is less a criticism and more a recognition that in the age of the white self-sufficient man, preaching struggles to turn us toward the Spirit. That turn returns us to the frightening reality of yielding to the Spirit, opening ourselves to hearing the Spirit through the lives of others, including our siblings in Christ, especially those of Black flesh.

Luke Powery knows this with a depth that few can match. As the dean of Duke University Chapel, he stands in the legacy of those who offer a gospel word in the space where town and gown meet, where powerful universities meet humble cities, where the academy meets the blue collar and the working poor, where the towering heights of intellectual life meet the streets—those who walk them and those who clean them. From that space, the deans of university chapels dance a rhetorical dance, asking the question: is there a word from the Lord, for places like this, for a time like this, for a situation like this, from a person like me?

The modern university is a strange preaching space, even in those universities born of Christianizing mission, because they seek to be secular spaces free of religious intoxications and provocations and yet open to all voices to speak their truth while being seekers of truth.

These are lofty aims that often avoid the truth of the racial situation. In many ways, the university chapel pulpit is a more intense reality of the American pulpit in this time of racial reckoning, where the urgent prophetic pull to speak out against racial violence and white supremacy can be quickly felt and easily resisted. To step into any pulpit today is to enter that urgency and the shrinking space for avoidance. Powery wants to erase completely that space, because he knows it does not exist for any Black man who preaches in predominantly and historically white spaces. Equally importantly, he wants to erase that space for the sake of the gospel that must be preached in alignment with the speaking Spirit.

In truth, the theory and practice of preaching has avoided taking seriously the racial situation. Homiletics has danced around this situation, much like a newly ordained preacher staring out pastoring in a predominately white congregation and watching their half-smiles turn into half-frowns as she mentions the words "race" and "racism" and "white supremacy." She then slowly backs away from the heat of that pulpit by escaping through a safe universal firewall: "we have all sinned," "we should love everyone," "we should fight injustice wherever it appears," and so forth. Powery aims to cut off every escape route for preachers and preaching, leaving all of us inside the work of truth-telling and dreaming. This is the doing of the Spirit, who gives us marvelous eyes to see.

Luke Powery wants us to see differently, to see the new humanity born of the Spirit. In this regard, this text enacts another crucial question, one asked by the wealthy man, Nicodemus: "Can a person be born again?" Is it possible to be reconceived in a more intense reality of eros, formed in loving expectation of life together, and joyfully received by a family not made by vain hands, not born of the desire of any man for the eternality of his name or his legacy, but a family formed of a multitude of different peoples with different tongues and different names? Preaching that is worth anything answers this question in the affirmative and in this way will dream Pentecostal dreams.

Everyone dreams, but not enough of us have the courage to constantly declare our dreams and expose the imagination that gives birth to such dreaming. Yet this courage is precisely what is needed for preaching at this moment. It is the courage to preach inside the dream and preach toward the dream. We must hear again Mahalia Jackson's advice to Martin Luther King Jr. at the march on Washington in 1963, as he stood on the podium: "Tell them about the dream, Martin!" But we must hear that command for us at this moment, spoken to us by the same Holy Spirit who sang through Mahalia Jackson, saying now to us, "Tell them about the dream."

These are not the same dreams. King's dream was a progeny of Pentecostal dreaming, a shoot from its massive tree. Pentecostal dreaming reaches beyond the hopes of any nation-state, and grasps a more radical belonging, one that joins us in a shared vision of God made flesh, and at work in our flesh, reflecting divine glory between us and binding us together in common cause for creating thriving life. King's dream has gone unanswered because we live in a racial world that resists the Spirit's calling. Yet such resistance can never be the last word for those who breathe in Pentecostal wind and breathe out hope.

Hopeless preaching is an oxymoron, but those who refuse to preach into the racial crisis, through to the hope of a new humanity beyond the racial condition, engage in such oxymoronic speech. They resist the Spirit and have lost sight of their own humanity. The Spirit, however, will not be thwarted by our resistance, because there are always those who yield to the flow of God and thereby become sources for streams of living water. Indeed, there is no better definition of an anti-racist preaching life than this: to become a source for streams of living water. This is the doing of the Spirit, who gives us marvelous eyes to see.

Willie James Jennings
Hamden, Connecticut

Prelude

Let Us Break Bread Together

During the spring semester of 2020, I was on sabbatical from Duke University and gave the Thomas White Currie Lectures at Austin Presbyterian Theological Seminary in Austin, Texas, in February of that year. The theme of my three lectures was "Searching for Common Ground." This book is the expanded fruit from those three literary-theological branches, and I am forever grateful to President Ted Wardlaw for his invitation and to the Austin Seminary community for their hospitality. Only a little more than a month later, a global pandemic—COVID-19—would strike the world, changing the way of life as we know it. If that was not enough, a couple of months later, a Black man, George Floyd, was tragically killed in police custody, sparking protests all over the nation and world. It was a reminder of the pandemic of racism that had long infected US society. This older pandemic raised its head in Minneapolis for all the world to see as we watched Floyd's head being pinned to the ground by a knee. That knee on a neck kneed the spirit, the breath of life, out of another human being. It was a horrific visual reminder that being born in the USA does not mean belonging in the USA. The convergence of a health and racial pandemic created a kind of pandemonium, a word rightly reserved for the name of the capital of hell in John Milton's epic poem *Paradise Lost.*

All of the physical and social death, all of the hell, of 2020 up to now is the context for this writing endeavor, a time at which many are stripped of the usual accoutrements and perhaps realize for the first time the naked reality of our mortality and humanity. But at the same time, there is an irony of the human condition at play. It can seem that we are closer to technology than one another. We can go to space and not make space for each other. Maybe this is the real pandemonium of our time and why this book yearns, sighs, for human togetherness and a different way of thinking of and engaging one another with the help of the Spirit, such that "racing" ends and embracing begins.

I have been helped by the Spirit all throughout my life's journey, but I have also been accompanied by human beings who have chosen to walk alongside me, professionally and personally. In many ways, even if they do not use this language, their presence has been a "ministry with humanity" toward me. I am particularly grateful to Duke University president Vincent Price, who approved the sabbatical that enabled me to have focused research and writing time. But the truth is that I would not have taken a sabbatical in the first place if my Duke Chapel colleagues, Amanda Hughes and Bruce Puckett, were not willing to take on more leadership responsibilities during my absence. I want to commend the amazing job they did guiding the chapel community as a whole through the onset of COVID-19.

I would be remiss if I did not thank the entire Duke Chapel community and my divinity school colleagues and students who raise probing questions and are willing to wrestle with God until a blessing comes. It is true as one of my colleagues has said of the chapel—it is an "odd assortment" of people, but it is this oddity that reflects the profundity of the gospel for all flesh.

To be honest, it may also seem odd—as a Duke Blue Devil—that on my sabbatical I had an appointment as a visiting associate professor in Carolina Tarheel land at UNC–Chapel Hill in the African, African American, and Diaspora Studies Department in the College of Arts and Sciences. Eunice Sahle, chair of the department at the time, welcomed me so warmly, even though my time was cut short due to the onset of the pandemic. Despite the brevity of my time there, we were able to share with one another our mutual admiration for Howard Thurman.

Of course, no book is written in a vacuum. There are so many intellectual influences, guides, and interlocutors, whether in the academy, church, or the broader society. Yet this work in particular is better because of the heads and hearts of two specific homiletics colleagues and friends: Kenyatta Gilbert and Paul Scott Wilson, who read chapter drafts and whose insights and questions helped the ideas in this book to be more cohesive, clear, and generative. The editorial genius of Bob Ratcliff, editor-in-chief at Westminster John Knox, also made this book more fruitful and useful for the church and theological education; I thank him for his ongoing support throughout the years. In addition, my assistant, Ava West, provided tremendous support and work on footnote details; without her, this book would not have been completed on time. For the grace, poise, and kindness with which she coordinates much of my communication and schedule, I am deeply grateful.

My heartfelt thanks continue as I lift praises for the foreword by Yale professor and former Duke colleague Willie Jennings, who, by writing, gave a generous gift of time, energy, mind, and heart; his words are linguistic icons to the deep wellspring of God's wisdom and presence.

Furthermore, my gratitude overflows into song as I remember the kindness, commitment, love, and faith of my family that has shaped my humanity, specifically my wife, Gail, and our two children, Moriah and Zachary. They make space for the Spirit that I might have space to write in the Spirit on such topics as the one in this book.

The mention of these names (and there are more) is like a genealogy that speaks of the origins of this work while indicating that I am not alone in life nor in this endeavor. Rather, I am surrounded by a great cloud of witnesses who cheer me on in scholarship, ministry, and life. These human beings make me more fully human.

However, none of this is possible without the gracious God who became human in Jesus Christ and breathes the life of the Spirit on us that we may live more abundantly and humanly. And thus I say, like J. S. Bach, *Soli Deo Gloria*.

Luke A. Powery

Introduction

Wade in the Water

Wade in the water, God's a-gonna trouble the water.
—Spiritual

For in the one Spirit we were all baptized into one body—Jews or Greeks, slaves or free—and we were all made to drink of one Spirit.
—1 Corinthians 12:13

[E]very human being is an unprecedented miracle. One tries to treat them as the miracles they are, while trying to protect oneself against the disasters they've become.
—James Baldwin[1]

A STORY OF BEING RACED

I was born in the Bronx, New York, and grew up in Miami, Florida, both cosmopolitan cities with a wide range of human hues and life situations. But even with the makeup of a mosaic of sorts in these cities, a type of cosmos on earth, there was often a concern with skin color, and sometimes one was on the right side of the racial tracks, and at other times, the wrong. In this context, over the years an explicit question was often posed to other family members and me: What color are you?

Where I grew up in Miami during my adolescent years, there were particular school days focused informally on certain races or colors of people, and depending on the designated day, one had to be careful. There were specific days to exert violence on white people and other days to pound the flesh of Black people. One afternoon, I was on the middle school basketball court outside, waiting for baseball practice to begin. I was by myself. Three older high school students approached me as I stood on the court. I sensed what was up: it was the day to fight white people—but I did not see myself as white! I was "red bone" or "milk bone," for sure, as some of my friends playfully called me. I was a lighter hue of a blackness that ranges from vanilla to chocolate skin

1. James Baldwin, *The Price of the Ticket: Collected Nonfiction, 1948–1985* (Boston: Beacon, 1985), 453.

1

tones. Yet these three older teenagers did not see what I knew; they judged a human book by its cover. They were ready for a fight although "no one ever wins a fight."[2] They surrounded me as I watched their slow, intentional movement. One of them raised a question: "What color is your mother?" I responded, "Black." That same older student replied, "Ding, ding, ding. Saved by the bell." And they walked away. My answer satisfied their racialized query but also reminded me of what the elders have taught: skin folk are not always kinfolk.

What color is your mother? What color are you? Why did that matter? Why was this so important to these three high schoolers? What sort of psychic trauma immersed them into this type of thinking? Underneath the question of color is the long, tortured history of race and racism in the world, a colonial inheritance and framework of a racialized human hierarchy in which white color is at the top, while black color is at the bottom. It is a raced question, one in which a human is viewed as object, a color, rather than a human being, bolstering and reflecting our "encasement in racial logics."[3] This encasement is a form of mental and spiritual enslavement. The social construction of race is a constriction of our humanity. Because of this logic, some are not considered human—only colors to be categorized, controlled, or cursed. "What color are you?" is an expression of psychological imprisonment that either enthrones color or kills it; this is how colonial racialization works. It destroys humanity, through either praise or rage, regardless of your skin color. There really is no human when the powers of racism prevail.

When Howard Thurman eulogized Martin Luther King Jr. in 1968 after Dr. King's assassination, he said this: "[Dr. King] was killed in one sense because [hu]mankind is not quite human yet. May he live because all of us in America are closer to becoming human than ever before."[4] Thurman suggests that being human has something to do with nonviolence and nurturing and affirming the life of others, because racism and racialization dehumanize people and destroy them, as in the case of Dr. King. We are "not quite human yet" because of ongoing racialized violence against each other. We get "closer to becoming human" when

2. Howard Thurman's grandmother Nancy Ambrose told this to him after he had a fight with a classmate. See Howard Thurman, *With Head and Heart: The Autobiography of Howard Thurman* (Orlando, FL: Harvest, 1979), 12.

3. Willie James Jennings, *The Christian Imagination: Theology and the Origins of Race* (New Haven, CT: Yale University Press, 2010), 8.

4. Howard Thurman, "Litany and Words in Memoriam: Martin Luther King, Jr.," April 7, 1968, https://www.bu.edu/htpp/files/2017/06/1968-4-07-Litany-Words-in-Memoriam-of-MLK.pdf.

those who are the racialized other live and do not die because they have been raced. This racialized reality, especially for Black men, leads Imani Perry to write her sons a letter called *Breathe*, in which she says, "I have known from the very first day of each of your lives that I cannot guarantee your safety."[5]

The threat of violence against someone because of the color of their skin is real. To be raced is often to be erased from the sphere of humanity, to be othered. The other "exist[s] beyond the border of a great 'belonging.'"[6] By racialization some human beings are made not to belong. They are raced by a lust for power and control, rather than affirmed as human and holy by the Spirit's breath. To be or become more fully human is a challenge in an inhumane world. But it is a struggle, a wrestling, that is worth it, even in stormy waters. This book wades into these racialized waters because in the Spirit, God's a-gonna trouble the water.

INHABITING A RACED WORLD AND CHURCH

Although certain segments of the broader society may argue that racism no longer exists, this project does not engage that debate but functions with the understanding that racism is real in powerful, enfleshed ways in the world and the church. Race is an idea, a social construct, not a biological reality, yet it has social power and shapes the world.[7] This ideological construct racializes the world. Remember, "racism precedes race."[8] Thus, the world and the church are raced because of death-wielding racist ideals. "Race is the structure of death, the dehumanizing and de-creating word a people sought to speak over the world, and violently succeeded."[9] Colonial powers, including the

---

5. Imani Perry, *Breathe: A Letter to My Sons* (Boston: Beacon, 2019), 8.

6. Ta-Nehisi Coates, "Foreword," in Toni Morrison, *The Origin of Others* (Cambridge, MA: Harvard University Press, 2017), xv.

7. There are many works on the history of race and racism in the world. A few examples are Eduardo Bonilla-Silva, *Racism without Racists: Color-Blind Racism and the Persistence of Racial Inequality in the United States* (Lanham, MD: Rowman & Littlefield, 2010); John Hope Franklin, *From Slavery to Freedom: A History of African Americans*, 8th ed. (New York: Knopf, 2006); George M. Frederickson, *Racism: A Short History* (Princeton, NJ: Princeton University Press, 2002); and Ibram X. Kendi, *Stamped from the Beginning: The Definitive History of Racist Ideas in America* (New York: Bold Type, 2016).

8. Coates, "Foreword," xi.

9. Brian Bantum, *The Death of Race: Building a New Christianity in a Racial World* (Minneapolis: Fortress, 2016), 14.

United States, enacted racialization as a global imperial project, which causes Duke sociology professor Eduardo Bonilla-Silva to write, "Racial considerations shade almost everything in America."[10] From slavery to Reconstruction, the Jim Crow era, the civil rights movement, and legalized desegregation, the United States is racialized, and there is no escaping it. It is "in the 'national' character."[11]

But one must acknowledge there is often confusion around terminology and definitions for words such as "race," "racism," and "racial," while others shy away from even using color terms, such as black or white, to describe human beings, because it might feed into the belief that race is biological when it is not. Others prefer to highlight ancestral roots and use "African American" or "European American" or "Latin American," as examples. There is no one-size-fits-all, linguistically. As the book *How Real Is Race?* asserts about the discourse on race, "it's a semantic mess."[12] Terms can be messy and muddy the waters of understanding; however, while race is neither biologically nor ontologically real, it is *socially* real. Thus, throughout this book I will use the term "racialization" predominantly to emphasize how race is something that is performed on another person or group. Racialization is real. A person or group can be raced or racialized. In this way, one uses "race" to objectify and control another. Racialization leading to dehumanization has been the historical manifestation of race.

Tied to this semantic confusion is another term, "whiteness." People get offended often because they believe it is a biological term, referring to all white-colored people across time. But I adhere to the insightful perspective and teaching of Willie Jennings, who writes that it "does not refer to people of European descent but to a way of being in the world and seeing the world that forms cognitive and affective structures able to seduce people into its habitation and its meaning making."[13] "It is a way of organizing life,"[14] and as Jemar Tisby points out, it "isn't

---

10. Bonilla-Silva, *Racism without Racists*, 2. His sociological work confronts those who might argue racism no longer exists through his research on color-blind racism.

11. Toni Morrison, *Playing in the Dark: Whiteness and the Literary Imagination* (Cambridge, MA: Harvard University Press, 1992), 63.

12. Carol C. Mukhopadhyay, Rosemary Henze, and Yolanda T. Moses, *How Real Is Race? A Sourcebook on Race, Culture, and Biology* (Lanham, MD: Rowman & Littlefield, 2014), xxii. For more about defining race-related terms, see Bonilla-Silva, *Racism without Racists*, 8–10.

13. Willie James Jennings, *After Whiteness: An Education in Belonging* (Grand Rapids: Eerdmans, 2020), 9.

14. Jennings, *After Whiteness*, 8.

a matter of melanin, it's a matter of power."[15] Racialization perpetuated by whiteness has historically been about the power to control and destroy, racing that which needs to be dominated because it is perceived to be in the way, economically, socially, or even religiously.

The struggle to define is important, but we ought to be careful that it does not distract from the fact that "[w]alls are going up around the world to keep people separated from one another. . . . The process of colonization that robbed some of land and language for centuries and which divided people according to such categories continues to rob people of their dignity and lives in the present."[16] This is the key point and understanding in this book: human division and polarization perpetrate injustices that undercut the dignity of all people, but especially those thrust to the margins by racialization. And to be clear, the church has been as complicit in racism, and as raced, as the world.

It has been said that the most segregated hour in America is 11 a.m. on Sunday, when churches gather.[17] This reality is a reflection of history, the unfortunate history of Christianity's baptism of the enslavement of Black peoples and the historical oppression of the other across the world. "Racism continues to plague the church,"[18] and silence, evasion, and indifference are not faithful Christian options. Thus, this book is geared toward the church and is an attempt to lure the church out of indifference, into meaningful engagement and hopeful opportunities in relation to raced relations, systems, and structures.

Of all the organized entities, the church should be focused on and working toward the flourishing of all human beings on earth, rooted in the incarnation of God in Jesus Christ, who came to earth as a human being. However, what has happened historically in this raced environment, of which the church has been a part, is that barely any room has been cultivated in either the world or the church for becoming human in the fullest sense, because some people have been viewed not as people but as pawns in a racialized game of power. More specifically, history demonstrates that there are those who desire the unbecoming

---

15. Jemar Tisby, *The Color of Compromise: The Truth about the American Church's Complicity in Racism* (Grand Rapids: Zondervan, 2019), 17.

16. HyeRan Kim-Cragg, *Postcolonial Preaching: Creating a Ripple Effect* (Lanham, MD: Lexington, 2021), 1.

17. Martin Luther King Jr., interview moderated by Ned Brooks, *Meet the Press*, NBC, April 17, 1960; https://kinginstitute.stanford.edu/king-papers/documents/interview-meet-press.

18. Tisby, *Color of Compromise*, 15.

of human flesh, especially Black flesh. To use the words of Perry, "How do you become in a world bent on you not being and not becoming?"[19]

The struggle for racial equality has really been about the struggle for dignity and worth as a human being—and I would add, a human becoming. Stories of this struggle for dignity abound, none more poignant in recent years than that of Ahmaud Arbery. On February 23, 2020, Arbery, a twenty-five-year-old Black man, was jogging in Satilla Shores, a neighborhood near Brunswick, Georgia. While he was jogging, three white male residents began to pursue him—two of them, armed, in one vehicle, while the third recorded the situation in another vehicle. They followed and chased him for a few minutes and eventually caught up to him and tried to falsely imprison him. In the resulting struggle, one of the men came out of his truck, assaulted Arbery with a shotgun and then shot him three times as Arbery defended himself. Arbery was killed, and the three men were eventually convicted and sentenced. Arbery was viewed as a threat in that neighborhood; he was raced or racialized, revealing how we are "not quite human yet." But fundamentally and vital to this exploration is to note that "Ahmaud Arbery was a human being, a person, a man with a family and a future, who loved and was loved. . . . Who knows what Arbery could have become. He was young, his life a buffet of possibilities."[20] He was a human being, but the raced world does not want everyone to be or become.

Racialization kills. It happened to King. It happened to Arbery. It has happened to so many named and unnamed, known and unknown. The church is implicated in the inhumanity of racialization, and it is time for the church to confront the racism of its past and present reality head-on. It is time for the church to remember that while we are human or at least becoming human, we can never be fully human as long as racialized violence still pervades the land, denying and destroying otherness.

---

19. Perry, *Breathe*, 52.

20. Charles M. Blow, "The Killing of Ahmaud Arbery," *New York Times*, May 6, 2020; accessed January 31, 2022, https://www.nytimes.com/2020/05/06/opinion/ahmaud-arbery-killing .html?smid=fb-share&fbclid=IwAR2iZchcOLIMxVcu0EdiLJfeuXOOKq5DB8GywSAsgHTQC2 p47fb4oai3Ru0.

INVOKING THE SPIRIT INTO THIS
RACE(D) CONVERSATION

This is where the Holy Spirit can bear some fruit. Writing the Spirit into this exploration is inviting the Spirit to come and blow racialization in another direction, a more human one. From the days of the early church, the Holy Spirit has been deemed essential for the church's life and mission. The Spirit is the one who empowers the church, the *ekklēsia*, in the book of Acts. At the Eucharist, there is the *epiclesis*, the invocation for the power of the Holy Spirit to come upon the bread and wine that they might be the body and blood of Jesus Christ. As part of the benediction of liturgies, one may hear the minister declare, "and the communion (*koinōnia*) of the Holy Spirit" (2 Cor. 13:13). Without the Spirit's blessing, there is no divine presence or power, no *koinōnia* or *ekklēsia*. Thus, the Spirit is vital for an effectual church community and experience of God. This includes how to engage conversations and practices around race effectively in a thoughtful, pneumatological manner.

There are numerous theological works on race that have been a luminous portal to new thought and perspectives on race in the church.[21] However, even if some of these mention the Spirit, pneumatology is muted and implied; we need to remember that one cannot discuss the Christ, the anointed one, without at least implying the anointing Spirit. What I aim to do in this work is to foreground pneumatological reflection explicitly for this exploration of race and racism in the church. The Spirit is often either forgotten or treated as an afterthought many times, when she is actually the power needed to overcome destructive dehumanizing powers like racism. In addition, sometimes Spirit talk is siloed within Pentecostal traditions; but the Spirit cannot be confined to any one tradition, denomination, or pattern. The Spirit transcends our constrictions and limits to transform us for the common good, because the Spirit cannot be restricted. The Spirit is a wind that "blows where it chooses, and you hear the sound of it, but you do not know where it comes from or where it goes" (John 3:8).

The Spirit is a wind, the breath (*ruach*) of God. She is a holy wind that woos us together rather than break us apart, because this breath

---

21. Some key examples include Brian Bantum, *Redeeming Mulatto: A Theology of Race and Christian Hybridity* (Waco, TX: Baylor University Press, 2010); J. Kameron Carter, *Race: A Theological Account* (New York: Oxford University Press, 2008); and Willie James Jennings, *The Christian Imagination: Theology and the Origins of Race* (New Haven, CT: Yale University Press, 2010).

blows in all human bodies. This common breath is critical for confronting racialization for a more fruitful future as human beings. Plus, breath cannot be raced. It has no color, but it moves in all flesh, all bodies, even raced ones.

Although this divine breath flows through physical bodies, pneumatology can be viewed as purely philosophical, esoteric, or just detached from earthly life. Some of this perspective is due to the fact that the Spirit is breath or wind and therefore seems to be immaterial. But in Christian theology the spiritual is material and physical. The incarnation of God in Jesus Christ was midwifed by the Spirit of God, showing how pneumatology implies materiality and the reality of incarnationality.[22] This means that the Spirit takes on earthly flesh and works in tangible, mundane ways. There is enfleshment in and with the Spirit, not sans Spirit. Thus the Spirit engages issues of race and racism and all of the implications related to these concepts and realities in material human life. God the Spirit is present with God the Son in the material existence of Jesus, and is therefore immersed in earthly, enfleshed life and is vital to a theological framework for confronting racialization and its effects.

This particular pneumatological emphasis on breath and bodies leads to the constructive pneumatological lens that will be used in this work to engage the raced world and church. My pneumatic approach to racialization will be rooted in the story of Pentecost in Acts. What is offered is not an exhaustive attempt at a full-blown biblical pneumatology of race. Rather, it is a provisional offering to continue an ongoing conversation about ecclesial thought and practice related to race. It aims to be constructive—even as it is limited in not trying to posit everything that can be noted about the Spirit and race—through the lens of Pentecost as a way to move the conversation further into more human and humane directions. This is not a perfect offering by any means, but it is one person's offering, and thus a human and finite one.

Pentecost is a helpful, intriguing story to engage the idea and imposition of race in the life, thought, and practice of the church, because that ancient experience has been called "the church's charter."[23] The spiritual experience among people in Acts 2 reveals what the church

---

22. I call this a "holistic material pneumatology" in *Spirit Speech: Lament and Celebration in Preaching* (Nashville: Abingdon, 2009), 2.

23. Theodore Hiebert, *The Beginning of Difference: Discovering Identity in God's Diverse World* (Nashville: Abingdon, 2019), 110.

is and what it should be, especially as it relates to raced relations and matters. At the beginning of the church in Acts, as the Spirit blows, we see what the church should be and what it is becoming, that is, a multiethnic, multilingual, mosaic polyphony of holy fire and breath, bodies, and tongues, all proclaiming God. The boundary-crossing Spirit of Pentecost shows the blessing of difference in whatever form. The Spirit of Pentecost offers a pneumatology that can move the church through and beyond racialization and all of the polarizations of our time. It offers a fresh gift of fire that can burn away the chaff of racist thought and practice among God's people. Pentecost can be perceived as "a clinic in the accoutrements of ecstasy"[24] but it is also a pneumatic canvas for observing the beauty and diversity of humanity. This is why the Spirit matters for this conversation on race, especially in the church.

The Spirit can help us reclaim our humanity with all of its rich particularity of culture, language, and ethnicity. A turn to the Spirit is a turn to the human race, not one specific racialized group holding power over other groups of people. In the face of the dehumanization promoted by racialization, the Spirit moves to humanize all people, especially those who have been dehumanized and treated as less than human. At Pentecost, the Spirit affirms all human flesh and tongues and gifts, regardless of raced status. This is liberating if we take what Thurman says to be true: "The burden of being black and the burden of being white [are] so heavy that it is rare in our society to experience oneself as a human being."[25] Racialization makes humans feel inhuman and more like objects than people gifted by the Spirit in their unique humanness. The Spirit reminds us of our human beauty that is wonderfully diverse. Humans are more than any imposed descriptive marker and are enfleshed beings created and loved by God.

Through this lens, the church has an opportunity to embrace people as spiritual creatures made in the image of God. God did not create the social construct of race; we did. God created the human race, human beings inspired and gifted by the Spirit. The ecstasy of Pentecost can be illuminating for the church's approach to race. Ecstasy means "standing outside oneself" and for this exploration suggests that the Spirit helps one to get outside oneself, out of self-interests, in order

---

24. John R. Levison, *Filled with the Spirit* (Grand Rapids: Eerdmans, 2009), 325.

25. Howard Thurman, *The Luminous Darkness: A Personal Interpretation of the Anatomy of Segregation and the Ground of Hope* (New York: Harper & Row, 1965), 94.

to see others' views and to get a wider perspective on God and life. To make human progress, it is important not just to be caught up with or in oneself, standing in one's own interests and identities. It is vital to stand outside oneself, as a means to make space for others to enter one's life. This is what happens at Pentecost; when people speak other people's languages and not their own mother tongue, the other enters in through the gift of a language not one's own. The ecstatic moment helps one see the world of race in a new way, from a different angle, even with a new expression of tongues. This is what the Spirit will do to show that "different" is not the same as "demonic"; those different from us are still human, always created in the image of God.

As creatures of God, "We are dirt, wet with Spirit."[26] The Spirit touches all flesh, washes all flesh, ignites all flesh, the human dust and incarnate dreams of God. The Spirit baptizes the material lives of human beings as they are and, by doing so, nudges them toward who they will become. According to Thurman, "[T]o be Christian, a man would not be required to stretch himself out of shape to conform to the demands of his religious faith; rather, his faith should make it possible for him to come to himself whole, in an inclusive and integrated manner, one that would not be possible without this spiritual orientation."[27] In other words, the Spirit shapes one to become more fully human, more whole, more as the person God created. Pneumatology thus implies humanity; this is why I engage a pneumatological perspective on race for the life of the church. A turn to the Spirit is a turn to the human.

Furthermore, the Spirit as a person of the Trinity has no color or race, yet the Spirit takes on human flesh, even flesh that has been racialized, thus dehumanized, in order to rehumanize God's blessed creation. This means that not even the Spirit is color-blind; she takes on the hues and colors of all of humanity by indwelling them, not to enthrone color or feed the raced imagination but to affirm the beauty of God on all flesh. The worldwide church struggles with race matters and their role in faith because of the legacy of colonialism.[28] Yet it is clear that the Spirit does not "e-race" anyone, implying that it is a part of someone's spiritual life. Deleting or ignoring color would be impossible anyway,

---

26. Bantum, *Death of Race*, 30.

27. Thurman, *With Head and Heart*, 120.

28. An example of this is discussed in John Burdick, "What Is the Color of the Holy Spirit? Pentecostalism and Black Identity in Brazil," *Latin American Research Review* 34, no. 2 (1999): 109–31.

since color blindness is impossible.[29] The life of faith in the power of the Spirit strives to make a person whole, including all of one's flesh, even raced flesh, for the beautiful purposes of God and human flourishing.

The vast work of the Spirit will keep the church honest, holy, whole, and moving toward racial healing and a new humanity. In the Spirit, the church can "de-fang cheap racism, annihilate and discredit the routine, easy, available color fetish, which is reminiscent of slavery itself."[30] The Spirit can move us beyond the objectification of human bodies and personalities to the recognition that we are holy subjects, free to live in the Spirit as one, such that every human being is of worth and dignified by the breath of the Spirit.

OVERVIEW OF CONTENT AND
MOVEMENT OF THE BOOK

This exploration of the interface of pneumatology and race through the lens of Pentecost will begin with the historical reality of racialization and move toward the hope of humanization through theological and practical reflection. Chapter 1 presents a historical perspective on racism, particularly against Black peoples, their bodies, and thus their humanity. It will reveal a perpetual history of inhumanity in which racialization is a form of dehumanization, through which certain people and bodies are not deemed human, rooted in the legacy of slavery but impacting the church, educational institutions, and the academic guild.

Chapter 2 will present a biological perspective on the issue of race, racialized difference, and raced bodies and reveal how the social colonial construct of race is not biologically real, in that racialized groups have been proven to be more alike than different genetically. By doing so, this chapter opens a path to the possibility of moving beyond the myopic "race" talk and the misguided practice of racialization within the church, to a different kind of theological consideration, discourse, and practice in relation to human difference (i.e., pneumatology), perhaps something that will be more fruitful, more spiritual, more Christian, and even more human.

29. Eduardo Bonilla-Silva teaches about the workings of color-blind racism in his book *Racism without Racists*.

30. Morrison, *Origin of Others*, 53.

Chapter 3 will draw on the day of Pentecost in Acts 2 as a constructive theological means for thinking about racialized difference and raced bodies, ultimately affirming the humanity of all, especially the dehumanized. This chapter will uncover new ways of thinking and talking about race and confronting dehumanizing racialization, inside and outside the church. It will show that the Spirit embraces all flesh, bodies, and tongues, as a humanizing gesture, resisting the historic dehumanization of Black bodies and people. This turn to the Spirit will be a turn to the human and begin to direct the church away from racialization to humanization.

Chapter 4 begins to flesh out what this pneumatological lens and emphasis on the human and humanization might mean for homiletics, the theory and practice of preaching. Chapter 5 will continue reflection on ecclesial practice by exploring what it means to do ministry in general with humanity, in light of the discussed work of the Pentecost Spirit and the thought of Howard Thurman, a person who ministered through and beyond racism during his lifetime.

Through the movement of this book, despite the racialized history of the world and church, I will demonstrate how the Spirit can move us through and beyond racialization toward humanization, a new humanity in Christ formed by the power of the Spirit. Pneumatology can be a theological resource to help the church move through and beyond racism to God's reconciling future present. Though there is a stark perpetual history of dehumanization, as will be shown, the Spirit's power ignites a type of rehumanization in which we can reclaim our common humanity. If "imagination is about venturing to the very edge of humanizing possibilities,"[31] then this entire book is a work in imagination, exploring the pneumatological possibility of humanization in our time, to find a redeeming rhetoric and ethic for how we speak and live as God's children on earth in order to become more fully human.

During this literary journey, readers will notice something about each chapter title. They include a haunting and holy idea and phrase from a spiritual, songs of the Spirit forged by the unknown Black bards during the flames of inhumane slavery in the Americas and other parts of the world. Each chapter, and really this whole work, is haunted by the holiness and humanity of enslaved African peoples, because they knew what it meant to be human together with other human beings in dire circumstances. Their spiritual sounds echo down the acoustical

---

31. Kim-Cragg, *Postcolonial Preaching*, 7.

corridors of human history and through these pages as a refrain to beckon us to become human in the power of the Spirit, even though "racial 'others' of dark complexion are always viewed as incapable of doing much."[32] They did much for so many of us and are remembered in order to re-member the future of the church and what is possible with God, even in the face of horrific realities. They are the unexpected holy guides for this conversation, not only because they are seers and singers of the Spirit who know about the struggle for their humanity, but because their dehumanized Black flesh is also the glory of God in human flesh. Through their haunting and haunted wisdom and life experience, we learn what it means to be not quite human yet, even while we strive to become human. Through them, we hear the melody of the Spirit's call, "there's room for many-a more."

SIGHS OF HOPE BENEATH THE WORDS

This expansive room or space of the Spirit in the heart of God is the compelling impetus for this work; underneath the words are "sighs too deep for words" (Rom. 8:26). These sighs are prayers of and in the Spirit, because prayers do not have to be spoken but can come in diverse embodied forms, like falling teardrops from human eyes. The sighs are prayers because the turbulent racialized waters in human existence are dangerous and treacherous. Wading into these waters is a calling after one has been baptized in the water of the Spirit. The unspoken sighs know that any progress in raced relations, systems, or structures is "not by might, nor by power, but by [God's] spirit" (Zech. 4:6).

These sighs whisper several hopes for the reader: that you will be willing to accept the honest assessment of historical racialized inhumanities and how the church is implicated in it; that you will learn that race is not biological but social and understand how this impacts where we are today; that you will discover a pneumatological way of thinking and talking about race, open to moving through and beyond racialization to humanization with a new tongue to speak about it and each other; that you will learn about initial pathways for how humanization in the Spirit can impact both homiletics specifically and ministry generally; and in the end, that you will see the need to move beyond rhetoric to an ethic that embodies the fullness of the Spirit of Christ,

32. Bonilla-Silva, *Racism without Racists*, ix.

to reclaim our humanity, and to become human with each other as the holy gift of God.

Beneath the words of every page are sighing prayers, whispering a hope that these ideas would take on human flesh in our day, as we remember the human flesh of those whose bodies have been broken by hatred and violence. I have a memorial on the right corner of my Duke Chapel office desk. Sitting side-by-side I have a communion cup and plate to remember Jesus Christ, and next to them a can of Arizona iced tea and a packet of Skittles to remember Trayvon Martin.[33] When I look at these elements, I hear a faint sigh, "Remember." Thus every day I remember broken Black bodies and the broken body of Christ, while remembering that at the Lord's Table, we are all one, which is why it is called communion and why we can give thanks (*eucharistia*) for that gift and eternal hope. Those physical objects represent the communion of the Spirit on my office desk, a calling if you will, that beckons me to a new horizon and new creation, where we remember every human being to re-member our new humanity in Christ.

To reach this new humanity means "that race must die, [which] is to say we must refuse the lie that we can exist freely while others struggle to be seen as human. . . ."[34] Racialization must die in order for something new to rise from the Spirit in our hearts and lives. My pastoral heart resonates with Thurman, who followed the scent of searching for common ground and yearned to transcend "the walls that divide,"[35] because in the Spirit of communion, we are truly one. I do not write about race to reify it but to "de-fang" its tight hold on the church and broader society, that we might be free in the Spirit to become human. I am filled with a "sober intoxication"[36] as on the day of Pentecost, intoxicated with an ecstatic hope for what we might become as human beings together in the wide circle of grace of a loving God. I am not drunk but filled with a new wine that has a flavor of the foretaste of a new humanity in Christ. Wade in these waters with me as we flow in the Spirit together and pray with sighs too deep for words that God would trouble these waters.

---

33. Dan Barry, Serge F. Kovaleski, Campbell Robertson, and Lizette Alvarez, "Race, Tragedy and Outrage Collide after a Shot in Florida," *New York Times*, April 1, 2012; accessed January 31, 2022, https://www.nytimes.com/2012/04/02/us/trayvon-martin-shooting-prompts-a-review-of-ideals.html.

34. Bantum, *The Death of Race*, 141.

35. Thurman, *Luminous Darkness*, x.

36. Levison, *Filled with the Spirit*, 336.

1

Many Thousand Gone

A (Perpetual) History of Inhumanity

No more auction block for me . . . many thousand gone.
—Spiritual

The whole creation has been groaning.
—Romans 8:22

"Color prejudice" is indeed an idiocy and an iniquity that must be eradicated.
—Frantz Fanon[1]

INTRODUCTION

Throughout the history of humanity, there has been inhumanity. Again and again, racialization dehumanizes. As Andrea Smith writes in an essay, "Decolonizing Salvation," "raciality is not simply a result of unfortunate stereotypes from peoples of different cultural backgrounds but the fundamental logic by which certain peoples are placed outside the category of the human."[2] To be racialized or raced is to be made a nonhuman, an object rather than a subject, not free to live as children of God created in the divine image. This historical logic is a reason to groan. This logic has not only dehumanized; it has enslaved and killed real people with real human bodies, especially those of a darker hue. Many thousand are gone. Human beings are gone, but their blood cries out from the ground, reminding us of past and present racial iniquities.

This chapter presents the racialized ways that humans have been inhuman toward each other. This inhumanity is not solely historical, though that will be mentioned; it is actual, even today, across academic institutions, within theological education, and in the church as a whole.

---

1. Frantz Fanon, *Black Skin, White Masks*, trans. Richard Philcox (New York: Grove Press, 2008), 11.

2. Andrea Smith, "Decolonizing Salvation," in *Can "White" People Be Saved?: Triangulating Race, Theology, and Mission*, ed. Love L. Sechrest, Johnny Ramírez-Johnson, and Amos Yong (Downers Grove, IL: InterVarsity, 2018), 44.

No place is immune from this social sin, because all of modern history has been raced, and there is no erasing of this reality. Before we explore pneumatology's potential for engaging racism and racialized difference, we must first tell the truth about racialization's history of perpetual inhumanity. Thus, with all of creation, we groan toward more hopeful visions of what can be in regard to raced relations. Though hope in the Spirit may be on the horizon, we groan first in the face of the racializing enemies of hope.

HISTORICAL INHUMANITY

Legacy of Slavery

The historical slavery of African peoples—and really of any human being—should never be forgotten. The modern institution of slavery was "terror,"[3] unjust subjugation, denigration, and dehumanization of Black peoples. Enslaved Black bodies, Black humans, traveled in the belly of slave ships on a bloody trail from Africa to the Americas known as the Middle Passage. It was in fact a messy passage, because some humans acted as if economy transcended humanity; thus did the slave trade generate tremendous amounts of revenue from the suffering of Blacks. This was none other than the "traffic of human flesh."[4] Speaking of this dehumanizing journey, Barbara Holmes, in *Joy Unspeakable*, writes, "Moans flowed through each wracked body" as "lament danced and swayed under the watchful eyes of the crew."[5] This tragic lament was embodied in blackness as a liturgical dance in a ritual of oppression and death. Historian John Hope Franklin writes that "many would leap off the ship into the mouths of hungry sharks to avoid enslavement in the New World."[6] Death was better than life. Suicide was viewed as a preventative measure against genocide.

Upon arrival in their new land, Africans "were reborn as property,"[7] not humanity, because of racist ideas. As property, anything could be

---

3. Anthony B. Pinn, *Terror and Triumph: The Nature of Black Religion* (Minneapolis: Fortress, 2003), 12.

4. John Hope Franklin, *From Slavery to Freedom: A History of African Americans*, 8th ed. (New York: Knopf, 2006), 39.

5. Barbara Holmes, *Joy Unspeakable: Contemplative Practices of the Black Church* (Minneapolis: Fortress, 2004), 73–75.

6. Franklin, *From Slavery to Freedom*, 44.

7. Pinn, *Terror and Triumph*, 70.

done to the enslaved, because they were categorized and treated as non-human. "American slavery unleashed an all-out assault on the black body,"[8] therefore an assault on Black humanity. It was "corporeal terrorism,"[9] which was human terrorism, because, as Shawn Copeland writes, "always the body is with us, inseparable from us, *is* us."[10] This racialized assault on the Black body deemed Blacks nobodies, nonbeings, chattel, to be sold at auction blocks, due to racialized difference. They were dehumanized and their bodies dishonored, as "the auction block left no doubt that slaves did not own their own bodies. Because of the slave's imposed identity as object, traders and purchasers did not consider it inappropriate to sell horses, pigs, and other creatures during the same auction."[11] For example, planter Thomas Thistlewood writes in his diary casually about sexual activities and rape of enslaved women alongside the shearing of sheep and other chores.[12] Black human beings were considered outside of the human domain, though ironically what really was inhumane is what was done to them by others.

Racism then and now was and is not only about genetics, but about power and control, the power to name what is object and what is subject, what is in and what is out, what counts and what should be discounted, what is human and what is not human. Racialization was linked to dehumanization. Enslaved Blacks were considered nonhuman possessions who at the liturgy of the auction block were "nothing but a body—a raw material—a zombie made by powerful acts."[13] But remember, the body "*is* us." What was done to the Black body was done to Black humanity. The humanity of Black persons was erased while their bodies were wounded and broken, sometimes by wearing "rope neckties" (i.e., lynching).[14] Black bodies, Black human beings, were deemed worthless and inhuman, even if, ironically, by inhumane acts.

8. Allen Dwight Callahan, *The Talking Book: African Americans and the Bible* (New Haven, CT: Yale University Press, 2006), 62.

9. Darnell L. Moore, "Theorizing the 'Black Body' as a Site of Trauma: Implications for Theologies of Embodiment," *Theology and Sexuality* 15, no. 2 (2009): 178.

10. M. Shawn Copeland, *Enfleshing Freedom: Body, Race, and Being* (Minneapolis: Fortress, 2010), 7.

11. Pinn, *Terror and Triumph*, 44.

12. Ta-Nehisi Coates, "Foreword," in Toni Morrison, *The Origin of Others* (Cambridge, MA: Harvard University Press, 2017), xii.

13. Anthony B. Pinn, *Embodiment and the New Shape of Black Theological Thought* (New York: New York University Press, 2010), 51.

14. Pinn, *Terror and Triumph*, 52.

Toni Morrison, in *The Origin of Others*, writes after accounting how enslaved Mary Prince was treated: "The necessity of rendering the slave a foreign species appears to be a desperate attempt to confirm one's own self as normal. The urgency of distinguishing between those who belong to the human race and those who are decidedly non-human is so powerful the spotlight turns away and shines not on the object of degradation but on its creator."[15] Whoever is different racially is demonized and dehumanized. Enslaved Blacks were "guided like incapable automatons," "pseudohumans."[16] In this context, the *other* was ostracized and eventually obliterated.

In this historical setting, Black human life began and ended with the bruised, wounded, broken body. Black human flesh could be physically marked through branding (a sign of possession) and whip-scarring (a sign of punishment) as signatures of slavery, making the Black body "scarred."[17] Enslaved Black women's bodies in particular were rendered "objects of property, of production, of reproduction, of sexual violence."[18] Through the erotic self-gratification of slave masters, female (and male) bodies were rendered sexual slaves. This system maintained racial and sexual hierarchy such that the "genitalia of these black bodies, then, was [*sic*] given extreme attention and importance over against the deeper ontological reality of blacks."[19] Blacks were deemed no-bodies, sex objects, dishonored and dehumanized. With this in mind, Lynne Westfield pens poetically,

> so many parts are missing faded damaged
> > it is difficult
> > > to re-member my whole
> > > danceable self.[20]

It is difficult for me or anyone else to re-member the wounded, broken, Black body of human history. It is scarred, and these scars continue today in a society in which "the black body is repulsive, hideous;

---

15. Morrison, *Origin of Others*, xiii.

16. Johnny Ramírez-Johnson, "Intercultural Communication Skills for a Missiology of Interdependent Mutuality," in *Can "White" People Be Saved?*, 258.

17. Carol E. Henderson, *Scarring the Black Body: Race and Representation in African American Literature* (Columbia: University of Missouri Press, 2002), 4, 7, 20–21.

18. Copeland, *Enfleshing Freedom*, 29.

19. Pinn, *Embodiment*, 83.

20. N. Lynne Westfield, *Dear Sisters: Womanist Practice of Hospitality* (Cleveland: Pilgrim, 2001), 98.

it encodes the demonic, the disposable, the lost, and the vacant."[21] For example, when officer Darren Wilson killed Michael Brown in Ferguson, Missouri, he reported that Brown appeared to be "bulking up to run through the shots." This is the depiction of a Hulkian Brown as subhuman[22] and the perpetuation of a history of inhumanity toward Blacks. None of this should be a shock, because within a racialized existential horizon, "the black *is* crime, wanton sexuality, evil, and sin."[23]

In a lecture titled "Caucasia's Capital: The Ordinary Presence of Whiteness," Willie Jennings speaks of Lupita Nyong'o, the Kenyan actor who in 2014 won an American Academy Award for playing Patsey, a female slave, in the movie rendition of the classic text *Twelve Years a Slave.* Jennings says, "Her accomplishment came at the familiar nexus for such achievement for black actors: when black artists perform blackness and thereby confirm their approved forms of humanity. We yet wait for the true artistic breakthrough when black actors are awarded this highest honor for acting the human just as white actors."[24] People of the African diaspora in the Americas have so often been denied full membership into humanity; thus, at times, to be Black was not to be human by colonial, European standards. On the contrary, Europeans were the standard for what it meant to be human, smart, mature, and beautiful. Through the racialized colonial gaze, therefore, whiteness represented the essence and epitome of human existence. The courageous, groundbreaking work of Frantz Fanon speaks to this. In *Black Skin, White Masks,* Fanon writes that "the more the black Antillean assimilates the French language, the whiter he gets—i.e., the closer he comes to becoming a true human being. . . . The more he rejects his blackness and the bush, the whiter he will become."[25] To be white was to be human. Anything otherwise was nonhuman, especially blackness, and was to be escaped, segregated, and ignored. One might strive to wear a "white mask" to cover up the Black body, because it was deemed unacceptable.

Black bodies generally have been viewed not as beautiful, historically, but problematic, an aberration, inhuman. The lingering scars of

---

21. Copeland, *Enfleshing Freedom,* 18.
22. Morrison, *Origin of Others,* xiv.
23. Copeland, *Enfleshing Freedom,* 17.
24. Willie James Jennings, "Caucasia's Capital: The Ordinary Presence of Whiteness," 4; https://divinity.duke.edu/sites/divinity.duke.edu/files/documents/faculty/Jennings-Caucasias-Capital.pdf.
25. Fanon, *Black Skin, White Masks,* 2–3.

the bloody, brutal, dehumanizing past shape the ongoing perception of embodied blackness as, according to Emilie Townes, a "grim aesthetic."[26] James Baldwin's father believed "black [was] ugly," which led to his own self-loathing due to his father's impact.[27] The influence of European Enlightenment philosophy is long and shapes the contour of human standards, baptizing white skin with all that is good and of God, while associating "non-white skin, black skin with unreason, ignorance, savagery, depravity, and mimicry."[28] This racialization propelled dehumanization of Blacks and their dismemberment from the membership of humanity.

This legacy of inhumane slavery and its afterlife can be difficult to remember and, literally, re-member. Often it is impossible to literally re-member the broken Black bodies of those, such as Sam Hose. He was a Black farm laborer in Georgia who on April 28, 1899, was charged with killing his white employer over a dispute about wages. His torture is described as such:

> Before the torch was applied to the pyre, the [N]egro was deprived of his ears, fingers and genital parts of his body. He pleaded pitifully for his life while the mutilation was going on, but stood the ordeal of fire with surprising fortitude. Before the body was cool, it was cut to pieces, the bones crushed into small bits, and even the tree upon which the wretch met his fate was torn up and disposed of as "souvenirs." The Negro's heart was cut into several pieces, as was also his liver. Those unable to obtain the ghastly relics direct paid their more fortunate possessors extravagant sums for them. Small pieces of bones went for 25 cents, and a bit of liver crisply cooked sold for 10 cents.[29]

Racialization leads to demonization, dehumanization, and ultimately, destruction. It is a history of inhumanity just because of racialized difference. Sam Hose was deemed a no-body who in the end had no body due to it being broken, dishonored, and dismembered. Sam was not just wounded; he was obliterated and tossed out of membership

---

26. Emilie M. Townes, *Breaking the Fine Rain of Death: African American Health Issues and a Womanist Ethic of Care* (New York: Continuum, 1998), 122–23.

27. Clarence E. Hardy, *James Baldwin's God: Sex, Hope, and Crisis in Black Holiness Culture* (Knoxville: University of Tennessee Press, 2003), 26, 28.

28. Copeland, *Enfleshing Freedom*, 10.

29. Noted in Copeland, *Enfleshing Freedom*, 119.

in the human family. It was worse than a crucifixion, because even his body was not left intact. It was torn to pieces, because he was considered nonhuman, inhuman. He was destroyed by the (white) lust to lynch that which was not deemed white, normal, and human. The irony in these situations is that the oppressor's humanity was propped up by inhumane acts.

Legacy of Christianity

This historical inhumanity, including the demise of Sam Hose and the many thousand gone, was also propped up and endorsed by the Christian church, which perpetuated a colonized demonization and destruction of the physical Black body, and thus Black humanity. I acknowledge this even as an ordained Christian minister, because it is the truth, nothing but the truth. Christian settlers in the United States believed they were in the New World by the hand of God for the purpose of "saving" those whom they encountered. Through colonialism, whiteness fused with Christianity, thus blessing "racial encasements" in which Blacks were reduced to bodies and the actions of their bodies.[30] They were not human, even to Christians. These "enlightened" Christians thought they knew what was best because *they* knew God. But what occurred revealed that they acted like gods, naming and designating people groups into hierarchical racial categories, stretching from white to Black, with the former being the best and brightest, and the latter being the dung of humanity. Christian people, missionaries, embarked on a mission through which they became the center on the throne of God. Thus the history of inhumane slavery is deeply connected with the history of Christianity, rooted in "the gospel of racial exceptionalism"[31] in which whites are the exceptional, divinely chosen race of people to exert God's will on earth. In this light, the church is "haunted by the ghosts of slavery."[32] According to James Cone, "theology's great sin" is "silence in the face of white supremacy."[33] This

---

30. Jennings, "Can White People Be Saved?," in *Can "White" People Be Saved?*, 27, 31.

31. James A. Forbes Jr., *Whose Gospel? A Concise Guide to Progressive Protestantism* (New York: The New Press, 2010), 79.

32. Copeland, *Enfleshing Freedom*, 2.

33. James H. Cone, "Theology's Great Sin: Silence in the Face of White Supremacy," *Black Theology* 2, no. 2 (July 2004): 139–52.

history of inhumanity was strengthened in many ways by white Christians. Howard Thurman's maternal grandmother is a case in point. She
was born into slavery in Florida. She could not read or write, but Thurman would read the Bible to her. But in terms of Pauline literature,
she would allow Thurman to read only 1 Corinthians 13; she told him
that during slavery the master's ministers would preach, "Slaves, obey
your masters," as a way to affirm the institution of slavery as God's
will. Christians, the church, perpetuated the sin of enslavement of
other human beings.[34] This truth led Thurman to write these insightful words in *Luminous Darkness*: "because a [person] is a Christian is
no indication to me what his attitude may be toward me in any given
circumstance."[35]

As it relates to the treatment of the Black body, it is important to
remember that the human body in general has had a tenuous role
within Christianity. In the West traditionally, the body has been
viewed as threatening and dangerous if not controlled. It has been
seen as unruly, with wild passions and desires. The body has been mis-
trusted and feared, especially the Black body. The human body was to
be disciplined and mastered, furthering a Cartesian gospel that contra-
dicted the embodied birth, life, death, and resurrection of Jesus and our
own embodiment, as if we worship God in "an antiseptic scene that is
pleasing to a deodorized faith."[36] The obliteration, the breaking apart
and breaking down, of Sam Hose, is not a surprise within a Christian-
baptized system of slavery. Nothing about that brutal historical scene
was clean or truly Christlike.

The obvious Christian devaluing of the body is intertwined with the
heritage of slavery in that Christian masters of slaves prioritized the soul
over the body. This prioritization leads to proslavery literature in which
the slave of African origin is in theory made in God's image, but "it
was the unchangeable blackness of the slave's body, which signified the
demonic."[37] The body, especially the Black body, was evil and worthless, especially for Christian practice and theology. The Black body was
inhuman, and therefore not worthy of dignity and love. "There was the
white body—the civilized, honorable, and beautiful prototype—and
the nonwhite body, most centrally the black body—the uncivilized,

---

34. Howard Thurman, *Jesus and the Disinherited* (Boston: Beacon, 1949), 30–31.
35. Howard Thurman, *The Luminous Darkness* (Richmond, IN: Friends United, 1965), 64.
36. Townes, *Breaking the Fine Rain of Death*, 173.
37. Riggins R. Earl Jr., *Dark Symbols, Obscure Signs: God, Self, and Community in the Slave Mind* (Maryknoll, NY: Orbis, 1993), 15–16.

primitive, dangerous, and ugly body."[38] The doctrine of racial purity and categorical difference and racial hierarchy rendered "black" as the bottom, as dirt to be stepped on, destroyed, and even mutilated. Racialization led to dehumanization.

This honest yet brutal legacy of Christianity was explored in an academic paper by Gennifer Brooks on "white preaching in the British colonies of the Caribbean."[39] She spoke of how British Methodist missionaries saw the enslaved in the Caribbean as "dark and helpless" and "mere cattle," who were given to "revelries" of "drunkenness, dancing, and immorality." Brooks notes how this colonized Christian perspective was an "erroneous analysis of African people that exists to the detriment of their personhood, their mores and culture(s), which were (and are) derided, devalued and dismissed as primitive, heathen, ungodly, highly sinful and even unnatural (where white ways are seen as normal, acceptable, and natural, if not perfect)."[40] This dehumanizing Christian legacy against Black bodies shapes the church and its ministry and stems from a "Platonized Christianity."[41] This history, according to Barbara Brown Taylor, makes many "uncomfortable in [their] flesh"[42] and, moreover, antiflesh, and as it relates to the history of racism in the world and church, antiblackness, anti-Black body, therefore, anti-Black humanity.

Black women and their bodies in particular have been sites of contention within the church's ministry.[43] The work of Lisa Thompson in her book *Ingenuity* and Teresa Fry Brown in *Weary Throats and New Songs* are helpful in this regard. Brown highlights the issue of women's bodies in the pulpit, since preaching is often deemed a male art form.[44]

38. Jennings, "Can White People Be Saved?," 38.

39. Gennifer Benjamin Brooks, "The Missionary Connection: White Preaching in the British Colonies of the Caribbean," in *The 2019 Academy of Homiletics Workgroup Papers* (New Brunswick, NJ: Academy of Homiletics, 2019), 243.

40. Brooks, "Missionary Connection," 246.

41. See Kelly Brown Douglas, *What's Faith Got to Do with It? Black Bodies / Christian Souls* (Maryknoll, NY: Orbis, 2005).

42. Barbara Brown Taylor, *An Altar in the World: A Geography of Faith* (New York: HarperCollins, 2008), 40.

43. Womanist scholarship and criticism have been vital in exploring the intersections of race, gender, and class as an avenue for a more holistic approach to truth-telling, teaching, and learning, with the aim of the liberation and flourishing of Black women in particular but all people in general.

44. Teresa Fry Brown, *Weary Throats and New Songs: Black Women Proclaiming God's Word* (Nashville: Abingdon, 2003), 9. See Lisa Thompson, *Ingenuity: Preaching as an Outsider* (Nashville: Abingdon, 2018).

When answering her call, Brown speaks of the opposition received and how the aesthetics of her voice and body were attacked:

> [T]oo much or too little makeup, too long or too short hair, too colorful or too dull dress, too low or too high shoes, too long or too shiny earrings, or too long or too red fingernails—was the source of criticism. My mannerisms were also evaluated—smiling too much, crying too much, speaking too loudly or too softly, being too happy or too sad, reading too properly or with too familiar language. There was a flood of criticism and a drought of affirmation.[45]

A woman's embodiment of the word has traditionally been the center of attention for critique. There has been a hyperinterrogation and objectification of blackness, but especially Black women's bodies. The dishonoring, denigration, and sexualization of Black women's bodies are dehumanizing gestures that perpetuate the history of slavery in our time. Black bodies, Black humanity, have been devalued, and historically, as just shown, a Christian context or theology makes no difference as it relates to the treatment of the racialized human. Again, as Thurman says, "because a [person] is a Christian is no indication to me what his attitude may be toward me in any given circumstance."[46]

INSTITUTIONAL INHUMANITY

Christian or not, this historical inhumanity is perpetual, because racialization floods the earth and many sectors of society, including educational institutions. Racism is in the air we breathe and in the soil on which we stand, wherever we may find ourselves. The historicity of raciality bleeds into our present existential reality. Universities, seminaries, and other educational entities are like churches when it comes to ongoing racism and the struggle for racial justice.[47] Though by no

---

45. Brown, *Weary Throats and New Songs*, 13–14.

46. Thurman, *Luminous Darkness*, 64.

47. For more about higher education in the South and its relationship to race, see Melissa Kean, *Desegregating Private Higher Education in the South: Duke, Emory, Rice, Tulane, and Vanderbilt* (Baton Rouge: Louisiana State University Press, 2008). For another important work about universities and race, see Craig Steven Wilder, *Ebony & Ivy: Race, Slavery, and the Troubled History of America's Universities* (New York: Bloomsbury, 2013). Several academic institutions have been reckoning with their racialized histories. For example, see Princeton Theological Seminary's "Princeton Seminary and Slavery: A Report of the Historical Audit Committee," 2021; https://slavery .ptsem.edu/the-report/full-report/. This broader context of higher education in the United States

means unique in this regard, over the last ten years or so at Duke University, where I work, I have seen—to use the homiletical grammar of Paul Scott Wilson—the "trouble" of historical inhumanity play out all over campus.[48] Because of my vantage point as dean of the university chapel, I am more aware of Duke's particular racialized history. Though the specific details of its history may be different from other institutions, the racialized issues at Duke are emblematic of the history and presence of racism across higher education. The church may be in "dozens of splinters"[49] but so is the whole world, including educational institutions. Duke, like many other universities, is an institution of the American South. As such, and along with the entire United States, it has seen ongoing struggles related to what W. E. B. Du Bois called—in his 1903 book *The Souls of Black Folk*—"the problem of the twentieth century," that is, "the problem of the color line."[50] As former Duke president Richard Brodhead said in an address to the faculty called "Duke and Race" on March 22, 2012, "Racial discrimination was once the official practice of this school, as it was of the surrounding region, and de facto, much of this land."[51] Duke, like many other institutions, has been infected with the disease of racism, despite its religious roots. The perpetual problem of a colonial racial hierarchy and categorization leads to the eventual dehumanization of the other. This racialization defines who counts and what counts and who is truly human and of value and who is a "problem." What Du Bois did not realize is that he was a seer, because this problem continues well into the twenty-first century at major research universities. The problem of the color line continues to color the tone of human relations and politics on campus. This problem, this tortured inhumane history of racism, ethnic hatred, and demonization of racial difference, still haunts and hounds our present day.

One might say that the dream of Dr. Martin Luther King Jr. is its own haunting echo, because his dream of racial harmony and beloved

reveals that Duke University is by no means unique in the various manifestations of racism on campus, although I focus on Duke because it is where I currently work and the environment I experience on a daily basis.

48. See Paul Scott Wilson, *The Four Pages of a Sermon: A Guide to Biblical Preaching*, 2nd ed. (Nashville: Abingdon, 2018).

49. Howard Thurman, *The Creative Encounter* (Richmond, IN: Friends United, 1972), 139.

50. W. E. B. Du Bois, *The Souls of Black Folk* (Chicago: A. C. McClurg & Co., 1903), 13.

51. Richard Brodhead, "Faculty Address: Duke and Race," in *Speaking of Duke: Leading the Twenty-First-Century University* (Durham, NC: Duke University Press, 2017), 131.

community, like Franz Schubert's Unfinished Symphony, is not yet realized. His dream is unfulfilled and may even be shattered, both of which Dr. King preached about.[52] "The jangling discords of [the] nation" have not transformed "into a beautiful symphony of brotherhood [and sisterhood]." The world has not become a context "where [we] will not be judged by the color of [our] skin but by the content of [our] character." "All of God's children" are not joining hands and singing, "Free at last. Free at last."[53] Society as a whole, including institutions, still beats to the rhythm of racialization.

There have been many individuals and some groups that have worked hard for racial equality over the years at Duke, but as Brodhead rightly and truthfully notes, there are at Duke "vestiges of the residual culture of imagined racial superiority."[54] However, to be clear, Duke continues to strive to be an inclusive institution and aspires to be and do better, as it works toward a vision of a beloved community on campus. Nonetheless, over the last ten years or so, various racialized incidents have occurred, revealing the perpetual history of inhumanity:[55] anti-Semitic acts toward those mourning the loss of people killed in a Pittsburgh synagogue; racial slurs and the N-word plastered on a sign for the Mary Lou Williams Center for Black Culture; the hanging of a noose outside of the student center early one morning on the very day Dr. James Cone, the preeminent Black theologian, was slated to present a lecture entitled "The Cry of Black Blood." Some of these occurrences caused an anonymous group known as the Duke People of Color Caucus to post:

---

52. See Martin Luther King Jr.'s "Shattered Dreams" in *Strength to Love* (Boston: Beacon, 2019), 87–98, and "Unfulfilled Dreams," https://kinginstitute.stanford.edu/king-papers/publications/knock-midnight-inspiration-great-sermons-reverend-martin-luther-king-jr-9.

53. See Martin Luther King Jr., "I Have a Dream," delivered at Lincoln Memorial, Washington, DC, August 28, 1963, https://www.npr.org/2010/01/18/122701268/i-have-a-dream-speech-in-its-entirety.

54. Brodhead, "Duke and Race," 133. For more insight on the history of the struggle for racial justice at Duke, see Theodore D. Segal, *Point of Reckoning: The Fight for Racial Justice at Duke University* (Durham, NC: Duke University Press, 2021).

55. Despite the racialized incidents, Duke's aspirations for greater diversity, equity, and inclusion have been made clear through various committees formed to assess situations and imagine a brighter future as it relates to race relations and the institution's recent commitments to anti-racism [https://anti-racism.duke.edu/]. I have served on four race-related committees: the Task Force on Hate and Bias; the Commission on History and Memory; the Steering Committee for the Center for Truth, Racial Healing, and Transformation; and most recently, the Education Subcommittee for the Racial Equity Advisory Council.

To all black students, staff, faculty, and/or Durhamites on campus and in the area: Please take care of yourselves and each other. This campus is not a safe space, and has proven beyond any doubt that it is a hostile environment for any and all black people.[56]

At Duke, there has also been the visible recruitment of students to a white supremacist group (Identity Europa) through stickers posted all over campus. These are just some examples of the "trouble" of perpetual inhumanities in higher education.

Harkening back to Fanon, racialization can also manifest through language. In one case, a professor had to step down from their administrative position after telling international students from China via an email to speak English on campus; the students were speaking their mother tongue in a lounge area, not a classroom or lab. In response to all of this, a dean apologized for the email from her faculty/staff member and assured the students of the inclusive values of the institution.[57] This type of linguistic policing is part of the racialized colonial intimidation that strives to maintain control and order of whatever or whoever is deemed nonhuman. These are examples of how even different tongues, different bodies, and different ways of being experience terror in our society, against the backdrop of whiteness. One is judged, questioned, interrogated, and dehumanized based on racialized or perceived ethnic difference.

These and other incidents of racial and ethnic discrimination caused a Duke student to write a letter to first-year students in the student newspaper, the *Duke Chronicle*.[58] It reads in part:

Dear first-year student,
We're not who you thought we were. We're like a kid caught with her hand in the cookie jar, except our cookie jar is an extensive history of hate speech. . . .

56. Duke People of Color Caucus, "Duke University, April 1st, approximately 1am," Tumblr, April 1, 2015, https://dukepoccaucus.tumblr.com/post/115190523116/duke-university-april-1st -approximately-1am-to. Some of the history of racialization at Duke that is presented in this section can also be found in my coauthored book and chapter, "Preaching at a University in the American South," in *Getting to God: Proclaiming Good News in a Troubled World* (Eugene, OR: Cascade, forthcoming).

57. For this story, see Sarah Mervosh, "Duke University Apologizes over Professor's Email Asking Chinese Students to Speak English," *New York Times*, January 27, 2019. https://www.nytimes.com /2019/01/27/us/megan-neely-duke-chinese.html.

58. Monday Monday, "Duke isn't racist: And other O-Week lies we've loved," *The Duke Chronicle*, 2018, https://www.dukechronicle.com/article/2018/09/180903-monday.

Hate speech here is like an ex-boyfriend from a bad breakup: our official stance is that we've moved on because we're too good for him, but there's still a part of us that keeps coming back for more.

The sentiment in this letter reveals that we are still in "dozens of splinters" and still living the problem of the color line, the divides across races and ethnicities; thus the inhumanity has not ceased. It still haunts us, and the world is hurting. Poet Warsan Shire describes holding a world map on her lap and running her fingers across the whole world. She whispered the question, "Where does it hurt?" and the world answered, "Everywhere, everywhere, everywhere."[59]

It hurts even at the front doors of a university church building. As noted already, the historical inhumanity of racialization and its associated enslavement of Blacks were blessed by many parts of the church. Thus it should be of no surprise what *was* at the door of Duke University Chapel. In previous years, Duke was caught up in all of the opinions, struggles, and actions over Confederate monuments, including the removal of the Robert E. Lee statue from the front entrance of Duke University Chapel in August 2017. The backdrop for its removal was the tumult in Charlottesville, Virginia, where

horrific, racially motivated violence [occurred] that began when a coalition of white supremacist and neo-Nazi groups held a torchlit march on the campus of the University of Virginia on Friday night, August 11, 2017. The stated goal was to oppose the planned removal of a statue of Robert E. Lee from a public park in the town. The next day, an individual linked to white supremacist groups drove a car into a crowd of counter-protesters, killing one person and injuring 19. . . . By Monday evening, the movement had come to Durham: a group of protestors pulled down the statue of a Confederate soldier that had stood on a pedestal outside the old Durham County Courthouse. [Then] the focus turned to Duke, to a statue that had stood in the portal of Duke Chapel for eighty years, unnoticed or unremarked by many: a carved limestone statue of Robert E. Lee, general of the Confederate Army. Although police presence at the Chapel had been increased, the statue was vandalized on Wednesday night—literally defaced with a hammer—prompting an outcry over this destructive act committed against the sacred building of

59. Warsan Shire, "What They Did Yesterday Afternoon," https://verse.press/poem/what-they-did-yesterday-afternoon-6524900794187889060.

Duke Chapel. By Friday, rumors of a KKK march and rally forced government offices to close in downtown Durham, as city officials feared a clash with counter-protesters. It was in this atmosphere that on Saturday morning, August 19, President Price wrote to the Duke community to announce that he had authorized the removal of the statue of Robert E. Lee.[60]

Religion and racial discrimination have joined forces historically and institutionally, as has been the case at other historically religious educational institutions. The church has been racialized; as a result it has also dehumanized other human beings. The church is not innocent in this conversation about racism, as already noted. What did it mean to have a statue of Robert E. Lee at the front entrance of a Christian church? What did it say about God? What did it say about worship and preaching? What did it say about who was truly welcome and who should be denied access into this human community? To me, a statue of Robert E. Lee at the entrance of Duke Chapel was a symbol for how the door into Western Christianity has historically been whiteness. This means that entering through that door was an implicit endorsement and acceptance of colonial ways of being and doing church. The Confederacy, through the image of Lee, was literally attached to the church. From this perspective, it meant that when you entered the Christian house of God, it was for the worship of a Confederate God, that is, whiteness. This Lee architectural symbolism at the front door of a church is hard to read as other than the endorsement of the worship of whiteness, not the worship of God in Jesus Christ, who was a poor, brown-skinned, Middle Eastern migrant, born in a Bethlehem barrio. The church is complicit in the history of inhumanity, slavery, antiblackness, anti-Black body, anti-Black humanity, and anti-other. Many thousand are gone, haunting us by their cries, the shrieks of Black and Brown humans who have been dehumanized throughout history, even by Christians.

60. See "Report: Duke University Commission on Memory and History," https://memoryhistory.duke .edu/report/.

HOMILETICAL-LITURGICAL INHUMANITY

Dehumanizing racialization is not limited to history or institutions, including the church, but spreads its vast influence over theological education and, in particular, the homiletical and liturgical guilds in both theory and practice. The subjects of preaching and worship are not immune from the influence of racialization. The Lee statue in the portico of Duke Chapel signals the perpetual history of inhumanity even in and through Christian liturgy and preaching. As it pertains to the theological guild, the colonial ghosts of homiletical and liturgical oppression loom large, though sometimes subtle. What counts as "the canon," "real" theology, "real" scholarship, "real" preaching, "real" liturgy are so often code for white. This has placed minoritized scholars and practitioners in a "ghettoized positioning" along a trail of tears within the theological academy.[61] In his book *Blackpentecostal Breath*, Ashon Crawley speaks to how theological discourse keeps nonnormative experiences and ideas marginal. He states, "It is the antiblackness of white theological thought that renders black bodies lascivious."[62] I would add that Black bodies and intellectual discourse are viewed as subpar and subhuman. A perpetual history of inhumanity invades theological education, though God's embrace of humanity through the incarnation hugs all human beings. A colonial, white standard is normalized in the guild and taken for granted and is thus invisible and preferable. So-called alternative thought is judged against this standard of what is considered to be the epitome of intellectual rigor; thus some may engage in a "phantom assimilation" or scholarly mimicry of a "mythical white male subject" as a method to reach the status of fully human and full maturity as a thinker.[63] Toni Morrison teaches about the invisibility of whiteness as a fishbowl that contains the fish and water. Through this imagery, it is the context for all meaning and sets the norms and categories for theological thought and practice.[64] What is not "it" is alternative, marginal, not integral to the core of human

---

61. Willie James Jennings, "The Change We Need: Race and Ethnicity in Theological Education," 40, https://divinity.duke.edu/sites/divinity.duke.edu/files/documents/faculty/Race-and-Ethnicity-in-Theological%20Education.pdf.

62. Ashon Crawley, *Blackpentecostal Breath: The Aesthetics of Possibility* (New York: Fordham University Press, 2017), 13–14.

63. Jennings, "Change We Need," 38–39.

64. Noted in Audrey Thompson, "Summary of Whiteness Theory," http://www.kooriweb.org/foley/resources/whiteness/summary_of_whiteness_theory.pdf.

intellectual endeavors. But "it" is never really named or made explicit. It is just assumed as pure, normal, beautiful, and human.

HyeRan Kim-Cragg writes of how this invisibility works in the academy, whether in homiletics or other disciplines. She notes, for instance, how rare it is for white authors to self-locate in their writing, whereas racialized scholars often face some pressure to self-declare. Racialized scholars' work is often seen as marginal to the core curriculum and perhaps relevant only for a small subgroup, not for everyone, whereas white scholars, who are deemed the authorial norm, are presented as teaching everyone, all people, all races, and all ethnicities. In this way, they represent the essence of theological education at its best. Dale Andrews once argued that "[w]e have not escaped the marginalization of studying the marginalized."[65] White homileticians, the luminous legends, even my own mentors, are often silent about their social location and whiteness, because it is just assumed that they are the premier human thinkers and writers for all people. Their race and ethnicity are invisible and normative, and anything compared to their work, or anyone different compared to their humanity, is seen as exotic.

The "real" scholar, the "real" human, is assumed to be pure—"white as snow," if you will—therefore invisible, and does not carry the burden to be named explicitly, because their racial status is the fishbowl for the water in which we swim. Blackness and brownness, racialized difference, are other, marginal to the mainstream of academic life, "marked"—thus marked explicitly on the page, as Black bodies were marked and branded on their bodies during slavery. The work of Black and other minoritized scholars is highlighted as an alternative theology, hermeneutic, or homiletic, as opposed to that which is deemed normative, holy, and human. Racialized scholars are made hyperpresent in order to be seen and categorized, thus made a clear target for marginalization and objectification within the human race.

We see the perpetuation of inhumanity not only in theory or scholarship, but in liturgical practice as well. Gennifer Brooks testifies in first person to how the missionaries in the Caribbean "changed the nature of African peoples with respect to their worship practices, from that of open and exuberant joy, to somber, sedate, repressed, and even silent worship." From her own experience, she speaks of the repression

65. See HyeRan Kim-Cragg, "A Homiletical Interdisciplinary Interrogation of Unmasking Whiteness," in *The 2019 Academy of Homiletics Workgroup Papers* (New Brunswick, NJ: Academy of Homiletics, 2019), 76.

of ecstatic outbursts, including the noise of clapping, the complete covering of women with long sleeves, long dresses, the naming of drums as an instrument of the devil, and the use of a hierarchy of colors where white was the purest and used to enforce a hierarchy of people.[66] Carolyn Helsel speaks specifically about preaching practice and its endorsement of racialization when she writes, "[E]ven if racism is anachronistic to the biblical text, the reality of racism—conceived of as a system of hierarchical racialized categories that elevated whiteness closer to godliness—received its greatest support from white Christians preaching on biblical texts. Beginning with justifications for the slave trade, white Christians have used the Bible to create and sustain racist practices and beliefs."[67]

Even denominational books that are to guide corporate liturgy have underlying problems. Claudio Carvalhaes raises the question "What is common in our common worship?" when he offers a critique of the process of renewal for the *Book of Common Worship* within the Presbyterian Church (U.S.A.). Carvalhaes writes that

> white reasoning has placed . . . minorities into the fringes of the *leitourgia*, liturgy, the "work of the people." We, the racially, sexually, and otherwise minoritized and minority people and communities are at the receiving end of this liturgical enterprise, turned into peripheral categories by "universal" white reasoning. We are expected to receive the wisdom of our white brothers and sisters, ritualizing our loves and faith according to the grounds of wisdom and tradition handed to us.

He does not want

> to dismiss the wisdom collected in the prayer book . . . [but to] expand the notion of what [is] "common": to open spaces for other wisdoms, practices, and thinking from people historically colonized and designated improper, whose liturgical practices and thinking are often considered "low liturgy," "popular," "contextual," or even "cultural" liturgies, as if the so-called universal liturgy were not also based on a particular cultural and contextual understanding of the body, of life, of race, sex, class, and worship itself.[68]

---

66. Brooks, "Missionary Connection," 248.

67. Carolyn Helsel, *Preaching about Racism: A Guide for Faith Leaders* (St. Louis: Chalice, 2018), 56.

68. Claudio Carvalhaes, *Praying with Every Heart: Orienting Our Lives to the Wholeness of the World* (Eugene, OR: Cascade, 2021), 76.

He argues that European colonizers othered nonwhites and "the stranger was to be de-negrated, turned black. Anyone who was not white was thrown into blackness, which serves to form and define the opposite side of whiteness." For his purposes, this includes indigenous people, Africans, Latin Americans, and Asians, and any *other*. He argues:

> The project of whitening the continent has been made possible by de-negrating, blackening, making a Negro of everybody who was not white. The blackening of people was a way to clarify and organize nonwhites into a lower cast of humankind by defacing their bodily features, sources of religion, culture, and forms of being human. Notions of white normalcy, control, order and so on, shaped through light and darkness was [sic] at the heart of this process. The creation of race was thus necessary for the creation of whiteness as an uncontested form of superiority and power control.[69]

His piercing question for the *Book of Common Worship* planners is, "What is the measurement of humanity we are going to reflect and put forward?" In other words, How broad is the beauty in the book? How wide is God's mercy? Carvalhaes asks, "If *leitourgia* is the work of the people what kind of people are we talking about? Who and where are they? Is this the work of the people we were or the work of the people we will become?" He even critiques a survey that was sent out because it did not take into account contextual and embodied reflection—human pain and hurts, racism and economic hardships of poor people—and since it imagined a world without racism and with entitlement. Who is "our people"? "Common" to who, for whom?

He weighs in on a disembodied methodology that ironically rubs against the understanding of *leitourgia* as the work of the people with God, but he also questions what "common" is intended to be—surrounded by the tenets of a certain tradition that holds that a white, upper-middle-class identity is a neutral, pure, proper identity that all people should aspire to assume, without attention to racism or economic inequality. What he reveals is that some bodies are peripheral to human liturgy and thus not fully included in the membership of humanity. He presses the *Book of Common Worship* toward a broader sense of the common and concludes, "A truly Common worship book

---

69. Claudio Carvalhaes, *What's Worship Got to Do with It? Interpreting Life Liturgically* (Eugene, OR: Cascade, 2018), 106.

would have to have a variety of expressions of diversities. . . . We would need to have a variety of understandings of decency and order that go beyond white reasoning where everybody 'other' must conform."[70]

Carvalhaes reminds us that there are liturgical canons and regimes at play in the life of the church. There are liturgical police in many congregations as it relates to time, space, the use of the body, language, and structure. These police control what it means to be humans worshiping God, and from this perpetual history of inhumanity, there are invisible standards and norms present that may never be articulated but are nonetheless real, a real presence. Certain songs, certain prayers, certain movements, certain bodies, certain colors are not central, not deemed worthy or human enough to be utilized in meaningful ways, except perhaps on "special Sundays."

PERSONAL INHUMANITY

There was a special Sunday at Duke Chapel in April 2014. The historical, institutional, homiletical-liturgical haunting of perpetual inhumanity became personal on that day. After the 11 a.m. service, I heard words that unsettled me and still haunt me. It was early in my tenure at Duke as the first Black dean of the university chapel. We invited Raphael Warnock, the senior pastor of the historic Ebenezer Baptist Church in Atlanta, to preach; Ebenezer is the church where Daddy King, Dr. King's father, pastored, and where Dr. King was nurtured as a child. One of his choirs also came to provide music for the service. This in and of itself was not really unusual, as Duke Chapel has invited Black preachers as guests throughout its homiletical history. It was a spectacular service with wonderful preaching and soulful music. People still talk about that service; overall, it was a so-called success. But it is what I learned after the service that has haunted my soul and propels me forward in my future work, ministry, and scholarship, including this book.

After the service, when I reached home, my wife told me that my daughter Moriah, who was twelve years old at the time, asked her a question during the service. She leaned over to her mother and asked her, "Is Daddy going to get fired?" What would make a twelve-year-old girl, after seeing and hearing blackness in sermon and song, ask this question? "Is Daddy going to get fired?" My initial response to my

70. Carvalhaes, *Praying with Every Heart*, 87.

daughter after learning about this was, "Well, baby, if I get fired for this, they don't need or want me here." "Is Daddy going to get fired?" No one had said anything to her, as far as I know, to make her raise this piercing question. To be honest, it pierced my heart, and I think it might have pierced the heart of many of my colleagues at Duke as well, had they known. I thought, "What did I bring my family to?" It was a predominantly white, Christian, mainline, worshiping congregation rooted in the white Anglo-Saxon Protestant tradition, an academic, elitist, university chapel that is Anglophile. This I knew, but I never thought such a question would spill out of the mouth of a twelve-year-old girl, my daughter. Her question has haunted me: "Is Daddy going to get fired?" Was it the soulful gospel sound with its distinct cultural harmonies at a higher volume? Was it the collective darker hues in leadership and an unconscious/conscious awareness of how communal blackness has historically been viewed as a threat? Was there a sense that an invisible liturgical, theological, cultural, racial-ethnic, denominational fence had been erected, not for dogs, but for racial/ethnic difference? Did she sense the white policing gaze and know that difference and diversity are often demonized and ultimately destroyed, so now Daddy was going to lose his job? It was a moment of proof, I believe, for what Zora Neale Hurston said: "I feel most colored when I am thrown against a sharp white background."[71]

The haunting echoes of my daughter's question reverberate in my imagination. "Is Daddy going to get fired?" The question raises the subtle, implicit ways racial and ethnic difference and other forms of human variation can be called into question and made to feel invalid, subpar, and worse, subhuman. My daughter's question and the particular context out of which her question rose confirms to me that Dr. King's dream is unfinished. What made Moriah speak this question? What had she heard or seen or experienced in her young life to say this?[72]

In many ways, this experience and question, along with the more explicit, blatant accounts of historical racism, tell us that, while scientific and technological advances have created abundance in our society, a "poverty of the spirit"[73] remains. That is, our technology has outpaced

71. Quoted in Claudia Rankine, *Citizen: An American Lyric* (Minneapolis: Graywolf, 2014), 25.

72. This story can also be found in my essay "'Do This in Remembrance of Me': Black Bodies and the Future of Theological Education," *Theology Today* 76, no. 4 (January 2020): 336–47.

73. Martin Luther King Jr., "Nobel Lecture," https://www.nobelprize.org/prizes/peace/1964/king/lecture/.

our morality, our spirituality, and even our humanity. In other words, as Thurman says in his memoriam for Dr. King, "We are not quite human yet."[74] "Is Daddy going to get fired?" I was not fired but have been set on fire to ignite a search for common ground among diverse human beings.

The long history of racialized dehumanization contradicts the love of God for all people. In God, every human being is a beloved child of God; yet throughout human history, those who are racially and ethnically different have generally been treated as less human than whites. Sadly, Christians have perpetuated this sin, although it has nothing to do with God, the Spirit, or the unconditional love of Christ. This perpetual inhumanity has been the fishbowl for centuries, outside and inside the church, and many thousands—like Sam Hose—have drowned or been destroyed. This is the truth, and the truth will set us free to be transformed by the Holy Spirit of Pentecost, because when the Spirit performs, something new forms for the world, the church, and human life together.

As this exploration continues, we will see that all humans, regardless of skin color, are more alike than different, nudging us closer to the mosaic vision of God for all humanity in the face of historical inhumanity. In his comments after the noose incident on Duke's campus, Brodhead, then Duke president, said "Duke may seem like it's all finished, but we're making this place every day, and we have a choice about what kind of place we're going to make."[75] The same is true for all of us. We have a choice about what kind of world we are going to make, and by our words and actions, with the help of God, we are making it every day. We make the places where we are. We make the world how we dream it to be. We dream a world of a beloved human community, one in opposition to racialization but in full embrace of humanization. This historical inhumanity raises the question "What kind of place are we going to make?" For God's sake, I hope it will be a human one.

74. Howard Thurman, "Litany and Words in Memoriam: Martin Luther King, Jr.," April 7, 1968, https://www.bu.edu/htpp/files/2017/06/1968-4-07-Litany-Words-in-Memoriam-of-MLK.pdf.

75. Richard Brodhead, "Remarks at a Community Forum on a Racial Incident," in *Speaking of Duke*, 219.

2

Oh Freedom

A Biology of Race?

Oh freedom all over me. An' before I'd be a slave, I'd be buried in my grave and go home to my Lawd and be free.

—Spiritual

There is no longer Jew or Greek, there is no longer slave or free, there is no longer male and female; for all of you are one in Christ Jesus.

—Galatians 3:28

Race has been called man's most dangerous myth, a superstition, and, more recently, a social construction.

—Michael Yudell[1]

INTRODUCTION

While racialization's roots lie in colonialism, its more recent history involves the pretense of a scientific basis. There was a taught biology for this racial ideology. But science eventually discovered and validated the truth that race had no biological grounding; rather, it was a social construction for the purpose of power and control in society. This is why I use the term "racialization" rather than "race" as much as possible throughout this book. As Ta-Nehisi Coates writes, "When we say 'race' as opposed to 'racism,' we reify the idea that race is somehow a feature of the natural world and racism the predictable result of it. Despite the body of scholarship that has accumulated to show that this formulation is backwards, that racism precedes race."[2] Race may be naturalized but it is not natural in and of itself.

This chapter will illuminate the faulty biological perspective on race, racial difference, and raced bodies, and reveal how the social colonial construction of race is not biologically real and is thus empty of theological substance and support. This exploration will open the door to a new wind to blow in the church and the academy and pave the path to

1. Michael Yudell, *Race Unmasked: Biology and Race in the Twentieth Century* (New York: Columbia University Press, 2014), 2.

2. Ta-Nehisi Coates, "Foreword," in Toni Morrison, *The Origin of Others* (Cambridge, MA: Harvard University Press, 2017), xi.

the consideration of moving beyond "race" talk within the church to a different kind of theological discourse about humanity, human differ- ence, and race in particular, perhaps toward something more fruitful, more spiritual, and even more Christian.

RACIALIZATION OF THE SCIENCE OF "RACE"

Most ways of talking about race are seriously flawed, including those that have claimed to be based in science. Race is not the work of genes, despite historical attempts at grounding racialized difference and hier- archy in science. With its complicated linguistic history, the term "race" was first introduced into the natural sciences by the French naturalist Georges Louis Leclerc, Comte de Buffon, in 1749, although people had been functioning in a "race-based" manner long before this, even without the official term. Leclerc believed that the differences between the human races were caused by climate variations.[3] It was an attempt to make sense of human differences by environmental differences, thus by science. There were also attempts to wed race to other scientific forms. In *Race Unmasked*, Michael Yudell notes:

> The race concept in biology can be traced to eighteenth- and nineteenth-century debates about slavery, colonialism, and the nature of citizenship, which were driven by the sciences of polygeny, phrenology, and craniometry. But its early twentieth-century mani- festation, in the work of those considered the finest scientists of the time—primarily eugenicists and geneticists—marked an important change. Whereas nineteenth-century race concepts were rooted in theories of racial distinctiveness based on measurable and observ- able physical traits such as cranial capacity and skin color, in the early decades of the twentieth century the biological sciences con- ceived of race as a reflection of unseen differences attributed to the then recently discovered factors of heredity, also known as genes. If polygeny, social Darwinism, and craniometry were the scientific backbones of a nineteenth-century understanding of race, then in the twentieth century eugenics and genetics played that same role, providing the formative language of modern racism. Hence, beliefs about racial differences became rooted primarily in biology rather than in social or economic ideologies.[4]

3. Yudell, *Race Unmasked*, 27.
4. Yudell, *Race Unmasked*, 2.

What this "science" of the day presented was the belief that human beings could be organized into distinct groups biologically, because each group had its own physical, social, and intellectual traits. The science homogenized the different so-called races of people. In the nineteenth century, anthropologists who studied both physical and cultural aspects of human beings began to measure, identify, and classify the so-called races. They accumulated data from all over the world on variables such as height, weight, skin color, brain size, and head shape, and produced a taxonomy.[5]

The progenitor of modern taxonomic classification was the Swedish botanist and naturalist Carolus Linnaeus, who devised his *Systema Naturae* (1735). He divided the human species into four groups: Americanus, Asiaticus, Africanus, and Europaeus. Each group possessed both physical and behavioral characteristics.[6] Based on the idea of a Great Chain of Being, which consisted of a hierarchy of humanity and life forms, his taxonomy judged who were the inferior and superior species.[7] "The problem with Linnaeus's taxonomy of people was that it was based thoroughly in what is now called ethnocentrism, that is, interpreting and evaluating other people and their cultures with the worldview and values given to you by your own culture. Linnaeus was Swedish, and 'naturally' assumed that his own people and their ways were the most advanced."[8] Later into the eighteenth century, German scientist Johann Blumenbach created five classifications: Caucasian, Mongolian, Ethiopian, American, and Malay. Blumenbach held that the Caucasian was the standard of beauty and all things good. His perspective was fused with white superiority. As Yudell writes, "And while racial differences were fast becoming part of the scientific vernacular, prejudice and discrimination based on skin color both preceded and complemented scientists' providing a vocabulary to racial ideology."[9]

5. Eloise Hiebert Meneses, "Science and the Myth of Biological Race," in *This Side of Heaven: Race, Ethnicity, and Christian Faith*, ed. Robert J. Priest and Alvaro L. Nieves (London: Oxford University Press, 2006), 34.

6. According to Linnaeus, members of Americanus were "reddish, choleric, and erect; hair black . . . wide nostrils . . . obstinate, merry, free . . . regulated by customs." Those of Asiaticus were "melancholy, stiff; hair black, dark eyes . . . severe, haughty, avaricious . . . ruled by opinions." Africanus were "black, phlegmatic . . . hair black, frizzled . . . nose flat; lips tumid; women without shame, they lactate profusely; crafty, indolent, negligent . . . governed by caprice." Finally, those of the Europaeus category were "white, sanguine, muscular . . . eyes blue, gentle . . . inventive . . . governed by laws." See Yudell, *Race Unmasked*, 26.

7. Yudell, *Race Unmasked*, 26.

8. Meneses, "Science and the Myth of Biological Race," 40.

9. Yudell, *Race Unmasked*, 28.

As noted above, racism preceded race. Science served the construction of a colonial economy that was "used to legitimize and justify the emerging global politico-economic order."[10] Science maintained the social order of the day.

Eugenics, the practice of controlled selective breeding of human groups in order to improve the group's genetic makeup, is an example of this social maintenance. It was spearheaded by Francis Galton in Britain and Charles Davenport in the United States. They claimed negative, deviant social behaviors, including criminality, were genetically based and connected these negative social behaviors with particular racialized groups. They applied these ideas about racial difference to immigration, reproduction, and other policies related to races.[11] These "scientific" ideas claimed some people groups to be unfit or debased; this led to the attempt to discourage breeding between races, especially between those deemed of lower and higher standing. There was even a movement to enact sterilization laws for criminals or the "feebleminded."[12] In the early twentieth century, Blacks were, of course, included in the "feebleminded." They were deemed to be lower mentally and physically, with the result that marriage and childbearing between Blacks and whites were characterized as "miscegenation" and declared to be biologically and even morally wrong for a modern civilization. Yudell writes,

> Through eugenics, genetics gave race and racism an unalterable permanence; neither education, nor change in environment or climate, nor the eradication of racism itself could alter the fate of African Americans or those labeled as belonging to nonwhite races. There were, to be sure, even in the eyes of the most racist thinkers, exceptions to black genetic inferiority. But eugenicists and other scientific racists explained these "aberrations" by noting that genetic material from white ancestry set them apart. W. E. B. Du Bois's success was, for example, attributed to the blood he inherited from his white ancestors.[13]

The eugenicists moved scientific descriptions of race from "the phenotypic to the genotypic," "from the seen to the unseen."[14] They

---

10. Meneses, "Science and the Myth of Biological Race," 41.
11. For these examples, see Meneses, "Science and the Myth of Biological Race," 40–42.
12. Yudell, *Race Unmasked*, 14.
13. Yudell, *Race Unmasked*, 15.
14. Yudell, *Race Unmasked*, 25.

stressed that race was not only about external visual difference but also about internal, invisible differences, genetic ones, that had caused the social or intellectual differences between the races. Racialized difference was presented as deeper than the skin. Racialization was grounded in geneticization. Davenport and others believed non-European immigrants, including Japanese, Chinese, Mexicans, and, of course, "alien Negroes," were undesirable and unfit for sophisticated life in the United States. Referring to segregation in the South, Davenport wrote, "For the present in North Carolina, I am informed these advantages are designed for white persons but for the sake of the progress of society, that socially inadequate persons with darker skin also shall be segregated and kept in happiness but kept from reproducing their kind."[15] Science was being used to solidify social order. Even the eugenics of southern physician and slaveholder Samuel Cartwright provides further insight. In his "Report on the Diseases and Physical Peculiarities of the Negro Race" (1851), he writes, "The black blood distributed to the brain chains the mind to ignorance, superstition and barbarism, and bolts the door against civilization, moral culture and religious truth." He even coined a term for a disease, "drapetomania, or the disease causing slaves to run away."[16]

The early scientific approaches mentioned above do not represent objective science. Tainted with colonial racism, they stoked the flames for a scientific racism. In other words, science was just as racialized as the rest of society. Frantz Fanon, in *Black Skin, White Masks*, writes that scientists "inscribed on my chromosomes certain genes of various thickness representing cannibalism. Next to the sex link, they discovered the racial link. Science should be ashamed of itself! Two centuries ago, I was lost to humanity; I was a slave forever."[17] Science was used to seal slavery and enslave Blacks in white dreams of dehumanization. According to Fanon, these dreams, grounded in a supposed science, caused "certain laboratories [to research] for a 'denegrification' serum. In all seriousness they have been rinsing out their test tubes and adjusting their scales and have begun research on how the wretched black man could whiten himself and thus rid himself of the burden of this bodily curse."[18] Clearly this was racism masquerading as science. If

15. Yudell, *Race Unmasked*, 36.
16. Noted in Morrison, *Origin of Others*, 4.
17. Frantz Fanon, *Black Skin, White Masks* (New York: Grove, 1952), 100.
18. Fanon, *Black Skin, White Masks*, 91.

"racialization is a process by which the marker between human and non-human is biologized,"[19] then eugenics attempted to give that marker additional scientific credibility.

Howard Thurman had his own experience as a little boy, when a little girl did not think he was human like her because he was Black. Thurman would rake the leaves at the home of a hardware-store owner and put them in a pile to burn. This family had a little girl who was four or five years old. She followed him around as he worked in the yard. She decided to play a game by scattering the leaf piles that he had created, making Thurman rake them up again. After a while, it got "tiresome" for him. He told her, "'Don't do that anymore, because I don't have time.' She became very angry and continued to scatter the leaves." Thurman finishes telling the story:

> "I'm going to tell your father about this when he comes home," I said. With that, she lost her temper completely and, taking a straight pin out of her pinafore, jabbed me in the hand. I drew back in pain. "Have you lost your mind?" I asked. And she answered, "Oh, Howard, that didn't hurt you! You can't feel!"[20]

This little girl thought Thurman did not feel like her, like a human being, and that somehow his biology, his gene pool, was outside of the borders of humanity. Scientific theories shape social interactions, as in this case, even though scientific bases for race have proven to be laid on faulty ground.

FAULTY BIOLOGY OF RACE

Since racism preceded race, as demonstrated in history, the idea of race is not biologically real. Thus biology cannot be genuinely utilized to ground any sort of human racial hierarchy through which racialization leads to the dehumanization of Black people like Thurman. In other words, biology needs to be "e-raced" because race is not ontological; there is no biological basis for racialized distinctions. Race is

19. Andrea Smith, "Decolonizing Salvation," in Can "White" People Be Saved?: Triangulating Race, Theology, and Mission, ed. Love L. Sechrest, Johnny Ramírez-Johnson, and Amos Yong (Downers Grove, IL: InterVarsity, 2018), 45.

20. Howard Thurman, With Head and Heart: The Autobiography of Howard Thurman (Orlando, FL: Harvest, 1979), 11–12.

sociological. It is socially real and is what influenced scientific perspectives on race. Anthropologists and others have argued that the racial paradigm, created by "science," of four to five races is not valid. "In a biological sense, there are no such things as races."[21] Race was used to objectify and control those considered inferior. Biology was used to naturalize social differences.[22] Shawn Copeland, in speaking about the Black body of Saartjie Baartman, writes, "The pseudoscientific gaze scales and assesses an object in relation to some set of [racialized] hierarchical standards."[23] Pure, objective science was never at work and can never be so. Race was ascribed to biology. The scientific thinking of race from the past, as described earlier—that geography determines visible biological markers, visible markers reveal biological differences, and biological differences, even subtle, influence character, behavior, intellect, athletic ability, and human worth—was socially constrained. The purported biological idea of race was not objective but "constrained by the social context" and "historically contingent."[24]

The boundaries between the so-called races are actually porous. Physical traits cross people groups. "Nearly all of the traits that distinguish human beings from one another are found in all communities, though in varying degrees. . . . [For example,] the differences in skin color between groups are only differences in degree, not kind. . . . Humanity as a whole is really a single, relatively homogeneous group."[25] This refers to skin color, hair texture, bone structure, and more. "Most so-called racial traits are continuous rather than discrete. The number and criteria for racial divisions are therefore arbitrary."[26] Proponents of biological racism did not teach that human beings across racial groupings are fundamentally the same, whether in relation to visible or invisible traits. This scientific teaching has held sway for years and still wields power on different levels, especially in the debates about intelligence across the races. However, even the American Anthropological Association declared in a 1994 statement, "differentiating species into

21. Carol C. Mukhopadhyay, Rosemary Henze, and Yolanda T. Moses, *How Real Is Race? A Sourcebook on Race, Culture, and Biology* (Lanham, MD: Rowman & Littlefield, 2014), xvi.

22. *Race: The Power of an Illusion*, directed by Christine Herbes-Sommers, Tracy Heather Strain, and Llewellyn Smith (California Newsreel, 2003).

23. M. Shawn Copeland, *Enfleshing Freedom: Body, Race, and Being* (Minneapolis: Fortress, 2010), 12.

24. Yudell, *Race Unmasked*, 2, 5, respectively.

25. Meneses, "Science and the Myth of Biological Race," 34–35.

26. Mukhopadhyay, Henze, and Moses, *How Real Is Race?*, 32.

biologically defined 'races' has proven meaningless and unscientific as a way of explaining variation (whether in intelligence or other traits)."[27]

The category of race does not account for genetic variation. It is instead the invention of colonialist biology, ruining society and social relations by distancing human beings from one another, when in fact we are very close, even across racialized categories. Scientists, specifically geneticists, have discovered that human beings constitute a narrow gene pool overall. There are "no pure stocks" of races, and across the racial groupings we are "genetically related."[28] This goes against the older science that presented separate races into hierarchies of being and worth and attempted to create a chasm separating some humans from others. In the documentary *Race: The Power of an Illusion*, a human variation test is performed among diverse students in a classroom. The test reveals the lack of genetic difference among humans. Test results show that only one in every thousand nucleotides is different across human genes, which means that under human skin we are all effectively the same.[29] The exterior differences are superficial, in spite of their historical power to shape social reality. What science now reveals is that there is more difference *within* than *across* the racial groups. One commentator put it this way: "[we are] more different from us than from them."[30] A writer speaks of this truth by saying, "More alike than different, more different than alike."[31] The most genetic variability is within groups, not between or across them. "Racial traits represent a fraction of total human genetic variation. Knowing someone's race tells us virtually nothing about that person's biology, DNA, or behavioral or intellectual capacities."[32]

The genetic closeness between humans, this scientific similarity, may be due to the "out of Africa" theory, which says that all human lineage, the entire species, originated in Africa.[33] Although there has been much migration throughout the world, humans have remained one species, not developing into subspecies or a hierarchy of racialized

---

27. American Anthropological Association, "AAA Statement on Race," www.aaanet.org/stmts/race .htm. See also Meneses, "Science and the Myth of Biological Race," 43.

28. Meneses, "Science and the Myth of Biological Race," 37.

29. Herbes-Sommers, Strain, and Smith, *Race: The Power of an Illusion*.

30. CNN, "Race & Reality in America," November 25, 2015, video, 1:32, https://www.youtube .com/watch?v=lL2VO_AVIgE.

31. Mukhopadhyay, Henze, and Moses, *How Real Is Race?*, 93.

32. Mukhopadhyay, Henze, and Moses, *How Real Is Race?*, 93.

33. Mukhopadhyay, Henze, and Moses, *How Real Is Race?*, 21–22.

beings with distinct physical traits, as taught in eighteenth- to twentieth-century science. Not only is genetic similarity compelling for a move away from racialization to humanization, and the recognition that all humans are more alike than different, there is a deep irony in acknowledging that all human beings originate in Africa, especially in the face of a history that has been anti-Black. To come out of Africa is to be born out of blackness; therefore all humans, regardless of their so-called "race," have Black origins. To be Black then is to be human, and to be human is to be Black, all of which flies in the face of a brutal history of antiblackness. African roots give human beings a common heritage, reflected by the genetic closeness science reveals. James Forbes writes, "Science suggests that the differences between the races are less than racism asserts, and anyone paying attention to moral behavior will find whites no more or less exemplary than anyone else. Virtue and vice, strength and weakness, intelligence and stupidity are evenly distributed among all races."[34] Maya Angelou's poem "Human Family" takes note of human difference, yet concludes that

> we are more alike, my friends
> than we are unalike.[35]

THE SOCIAL REALITY OF RACE

Even if biology is "e-raced" because race is shown not to be biologically real, it is still important to acknowledge that race is *socially* real. The impact of the historical biological approach fused with racialization of the other has shaped the perspectives on race in society today. Race is not biology but is most certainly sociology. Though it is basically agreed that race as biology is a myth and fallacy, it is difficult to abandon this centuries-old influential understanding of race. In particular, race as the valid subdivisions of the human species, through which a human hierarchy and chasm have historically been created, is false. Of course, because of this history, biology becomes part of the social invention of race; those racialized into certain groups socially experience certain biological consequences, for instance, related to health.[36] "Race and

---

34. James A. Forbes Jr., *Whose Gospel? A Concise Guide to Progressive Protestantism* (New York: The New Press, 2010), 83.

35. As noted in Forbes, *Whose Gospel?*, 83–84.

36. Mukhopadhyay, Henze, and Moses, *How Real Is Race?*, 20–21.

racism have biological consequences. But the concept of 'race' is an outmoded, inaccurate, meaningless way of describing or understanding human biological variation."[37] This all may be true, including how similar humans are genetically, yet race, as an influential controlling category, still exists. One can e-race biology, but one cannot e-race sociology.

This is the case because "culture creates race," according to Carol Mukhopadhyay.[38] Race as a category exists because it is socially constructed. It is real and impacts society as a *social* reality, not a *biological* one. Race has been a human-created classification that shapes social reality. This cannot be denied, but the concept of race is genetically defunct and scientifically vacant, because of the close genetic ties among all human beings, all of whom stem from Africa. Race, as inherited from history, is "an ideology to legitimize the dominance of certain groups. Race, then, is fundamentally part of a system of stratification and inequality."[39] Rather than a biological, scientific fact, in truth race has been a concept related to power and inequality. The racialized construct is a social construct used to control. It has never been innocent but was created out of motivations to dominate. As Coates wrote, "Racism precedes race." This suggests that race is in fact a social construction, not a biological fact. The work of Ibram Kendi supports this notion as well, when he discusses "the causal relationship driving America's history of race relations," that is, how "racial discrimination [leads to] racist ideas which then [leads to] ignorance/hate." He also astutely notes, "Racially discriminatory policies have usually sprung from economic, political and cultural self-interests."[40] Kendi reveals how other motivating factors, such as economics, preceded racist ideology. For instance, Spanish and Portuguese colonizers desired to exploit the mineral wealth of the New World and thus invented racial inferiority of the indigenous people of the American continents (and subsequently of the African continent) as justification for the slave trade and their economic pursuits.[41]

Race as an impure social construct also means that racial categories are not fixed but fluid, dynamic, negotiated, even reconfigured, and are

---

37. Mukhopadhyay, Henze, and Moses, *How Real Is Race?*, 93.
38. Mukhopadhyay, Henze, and Moses, *How Real Is Race?*, 98.
39. Mukhopadhyay, Henze, and Moses, *How Real Is Race?*, 98.
40. Ibram X. Kendi, *Stamped from the Beginning: The Definitive History of Racist Ideas in America* (New York: Bold Type Books, 2017), 9.
41. Kendi, *Stamped from the Beginning*, 22–30.

based on contexts, cultural, historical, political, and social. Race is neither universal nor inevitable. "A long-standing US assumption is that race, racial discrimination, race-based hierarchy, or something similar is a universal, pan-human phenomenon, indeed 'built into our genes' as humans."[42] But this, too, is false. Different parts of the world think of and approach race differently. For instance, what is considered Black in the United States is not necessarily Black in Brazil or elsewhere. Race is culturally conditioned. As Stuart Hall said, race is a "floating signifier,"[43] not permanent, and morphs its meanings based on the environment or context. Hall, like others, rejects the essentialization of race and the naturalization of racialization. Race is a cultural system and not "natural," or biological, or set in stone scientifically. Race "slides" and is not static. It is real socially and culturally, yet this does not mean that cultural characteristics are rooted in biology or that certain behaviors are biologically based.[44]

Yet, in the United States in particular, racialized thinking has shaped social structures and systems. This is obvious in relation to disparities in health, wealth, housing, employment, educational achievement, the legal system, and personal safety. These differences are not driven or determined by genes or biology. But the social construction of race has a great impact on human lives. Racialization has transcended humanization and has created and justified inequalities that people experience and endure. Though a human invention, the construct of race has dehumanized others because in this "racial smog"[45] of social history, various meanings have been attached to race that shape how people live, how people think, and what opportunities are offered to different people.

Race may be a social inheritance and ongoing signifier, but it has "no basis in biology. Thus, there is only one race: the human race."[46] To make this claim suggests that biological determinism is bogus in relation to race and that races are not real biologically; thus there is really only one race of humanity. However, a word of caution is in order, because many in American political discourse will use this truth of the nonbiological reality of race to deny its sociological reality, and

42. Mukhopadhyay, Henze, and Moses, *How Real Is Race?*, 98.
43. "Race: The Floating Signifier, A Lecture with Stuart Hall," directed by Sut Jhally, The Media Education Foundation, 1997.
44. Meneses, "Science and the Myth of Biological Race," 34–35.
45. Herbes-Sommers, Strain, and Smith, *Race: The Power of an Illusion*.
46. Copeland, *Enfleshing Freedom*, 12.

by doing so, perpetuate the falsehood that racism no longer exists. Racism still permeates society, as history demonstrates, even in the face of a nonbiological basis for race. Nonetheless, the assertion that there is no biological foundation for race rejects the long history of racialization and gestures toward humanization and the embrace of the human race of which we all are members. Even Willie Jennings asserts clearly, "No one is born white. There is no white biology, but whiteness is real."[47] He speaks of whiteness as "forming toward a maturity that destroys." Whiteness is not a particular racialized people but those connected to "a deformed building project aimed at bringing the world to its full maturity."[48] He, too, debunks race as biology but presents race, historically, as a socialization process to become white and disregard that which is nonwhite, especially Black. At this juncture in time, because of the inherited racialized history, it is practically impossible to e-race society and the influence of the social construction of race. Race is real socially, but this book does not attempt to reify it or give it any more power. It strives for another way, another Spirit, that might open the tombs of death-wielding racialization in order to resurrect a new life of humanization. As others have said, "Race is the classification of a species, and we are the human race, period."[49]

This means we can still talk about race but not in a biological manner, because it is empty. This is difficult work, because race has been discussed biologically for centuries, as if it was not a social construction—but it is. It is a social reality with a deeply unjust history. But theology, specifically pneumatology, may offer a new approach to this conversation, not one that dominates and dehumanizes the other, but one that embraces and humanizes the other. It is with hope that it might be a perspective to help the church move away from racialization to humanization.

RACE INVOLVES SPIRIT

Even with all of the above described, it is difficult to exorcize racialization and its power over society. It has a spiritual influence, if you will. There are other spirits and powers at play in perpetuating racialization.

---

47. Jennings, "Can White People Be Saved?," 34.
48. Jennings, "Can White People Be Saved?," 28.
49. Morrison, *Origin of Others*, 15.

Without diving deep into a biblical study of its scriptural setting, it is true that as Christians "our struggle is not against enemies of blood and flesh, but against the rulers, against the authorities, against the cosmic powers of this present darkness, against the spiritual forces of evil in the heavenly places" (Eph. 6:12). These principalities and powers and their activities are "the ethical context" of proclamation.[50] In his fascinating book *The Word before the Powers*, Charles Campbell teaches how "the powers comprise that 'something larger than ourselves' within which many of us often feel trapped and against which we often feel power-less, whether we hate or fear or worship that 'something.'"[51] Racism is like this—something within which humanity is trapped and in the face of which it feels powerless.

According to Campbell, this legion of powers (which includes racism) is material and spiritual. He writes, "The powers shape the spirit of human beings and the spirit of our life together in profound ways. In their *effects*, they operate not simply at the material or physical level but often most profoundly at the spiritual level of human life."[52] Racialization has been spiritualized and declared to be ordained as of God, and for that reason impacts the spirits of both oppressors and the oppressed. The rationalized-yet-faulty biology of race is one such destructive spirit; like all the powers, it seeks to dominate and diminish human life. Walter Wink calls this the "Domination System,"[53] which is "characterized by power exercised over others, by control of others, by ranking as the primary principle of social organization, by hierarchies of dominant and subordinate, winners and losers, insiders and outsiders, honored and shamed."[54]

Racialized hierarchy has been characterized by this "spirit of domination." "The lesson from history is that the dominant people of a time nearly always evaluate those they have dominated as being inferior. . . . Power, in the form of colonialism, backed up by a legitimizing rationale in the form of science, turned ordinary ethnocentrism into truly pernicious racism."[55] As we have seen, the so-called biology of race was

---

50. Charles L. Campbell, *The Word before the Powers: An Ethic of Preaching* (Louisville, KY: Westminster John Knox, 2002), 2.

51. Campbell, *The Word before the Powers*, 10.

52. Campbell, *The Word before the Powers*, 17. For more about how the powers are legion, material and spiritual, see Campbell, 11–20.

53. Walter Wink, *Discernment and Resistance in a World of Domination* (Minneapolis: Fortress, 1992), 49.

54. Campbell, *The Word before the Powers*, 26–27.

55. Meneses, "Science and the Myth of Biological Race," 43.

created for the purpose of enthroning domination under the umbrella of science. Sometimes explicit and direct, the system is more often implicit and subtle, yet capable of making its impact seen. This spiritual power of racialization is the source of what is called "racecraft." "Racecraft is a way of seeing, understanding, and reflecting upon our world, even when there is no rational basis for a certain worldview. The history of the race concept in American scientific thought reflects just this: the persistence of long-standing social conceptions of the meaning of difference in the thinking, theorizing, and actions of America's scientific minds."[56] This power, this spirit of racecraft, has crafted ideas and actions that maintain a hierarchy of humanity without any legitimate foundation other than racism.

Since this spirit of racecraft is so deeply embedded in the social DNA of so many of the nations of the world, but especially the United States, it must be confronted by another Spirit, the Holy Spirit of God, if humanity is to flourish. If not, the power of racialization, rather than humanization, will persist and continue to destroy any semblance of human community. The Spirit of God seeks to form a community of diverse and beautiful human beings, not for a hierarchy but for unity and equality within the human race.

There is another spiritual path, and engaging pneumatology will show this. For too long, the Spirit has not played a prominent role in much of the theological conversations on race and the church, yet the Spirit of Pentecost blows in a direction that might bear much fruit in the future as she affirms all flesh, all humanity, as gifted people of God. This is vital going forward, as the issue of racialization entails a spiritual wrestling, in which we struggle not against flesh and blood, the oppressors or the oppressed, but against the racializing forces of evil. Although people have been pawns in the powers' systems of domination that established racialized human hierarchies via distorted science, through the power of the Holy Spirit these powers can be overcome and destroyed. Toni Morrison once asked, "What would we be or do or become as a society if there were no ranking or theory of blackness?"[57] Perhaps we would become more fully human and not perpetuate a ruinous raced reality. The Spirit of Pentecost can pave the path toward this end.

---

56. Yudell, *Race Unmasked*, 4. See Karen E. Fields and Barbara J. Fields, *Racecraft: The Soul of Inequality in American Life* (Brooklyn, NY: Verso, 2012).

57. Morrison, *Origin of Others*, 58.

3

Every Time I Feel the Spirit

A Pneumatology for Particularity

Every time I feel the Spirit, movin' in my heart, I will pray.

—Spiritual

Your body is a temple of the Holy Spirit.

—1 Corinthians 6:19

Swing wide the door for the coming of the Spirit.

—Howard Thurman[1]

INTRODUCTION

As noted in chapter 1, Sam Hose, the Black farm laborer, was decapitated and his body parts were sold. "All the king's horses and all the king's men" could not put Sam Hose back together again. No one can literally re-member, put back together any historical human body, as we search for a more human and humane way, a more spiritual way forward in the church, moving away from racialization toward humanization in the power of the Spirit. Those bruised, broken, Black bodies are buried in the ground. Many thousand are gone because of a brutal racialized hierarchy empty of any biological or theological grounding. Human history speaks for itself on these raced matters. But theology, specifically pneumatology, presents us with a fresh opportunity to be, to speak, and to do otherwise than the horrific raced past and present. It can demonstrate that the inhumanity of antiblackness, anti-Black body, and anti-Black humanity is actually anti-Spirit. How can it not be so when the apostle Paul says, "Do you not know that your body is a temple of the Holy Spirit?" (1 Cor. 6:19)?

In the church, we can remember God and turn to the fruit of the Scriptures for this important study. Specifically, this chapter will highlight the story of the Spirit on the day of Pentecost in Acts, in order to

---

1. Howard Thurman, *Essential Writings* (Maryknoll, NY: Orbis, 2006), 50.

foreground pneumatological thinking about the racialization of human beings. The liturgical or historical significance of Pentecost is not unimportant, but I will utilize the day of Pentecost as a theological lens to formulate what could be called a "pneumatology of race." Through this constructive theological reading of the Spirit at Pentecost, I seek to answer this question: How might the day of Pentecost and the work of the Spirit on that day in particular help us think constructively about and resist racialized hierarchies and dehumanization? In other words, how does the Spirit move us through and beyond racialization toward humanization? Pentecost reveals, as shown in the following, that the Spirit does so through coming as a gift of breath, speech, and understanding, affirming diversity, creating a God-centered community, embracing all human bodies, and loosening all human tongues, in order to empower us to live as God desires. The Spirit is the presence, power, and gift of God that makes all the difference to change the world and the church.

THE PENTECOST NARRATIVE

For those unfamiliar with the story of Pentecost, here is what Acts chapter 2 tells us:

> When the day of Pentecost had come, they were all together in one place. And suddenly from heaven there came a sound like the rush of a violent wind, and it filled the entire house where they were sitting. Divided tongues, as of fire, appeared among them, and a tongue rested on each of them. All of them were filled with the Holy Spirit and began to speak in other languages, as the Spirit gave them ability.
>
> Now there were devout Jews from every nation under heaven living in Jerusalem. And at this sound the crowd gathered and was bewildered, because each one heard them speaking in the native language of each. Amazed and astonished, they asked, "Are not all these who are speaking Galileans? And how is it that we hear, each of us, in our own native language? Parthians, Medes, Elamites, and residents of Mesopotamia, Judea and Cappadocia, Pontus and Asia, Phrygia and Pamphylia, Egypt and the parts of Libya belonging to Cyrene, and visitors from Rome, both Jews and proselytes, Cretans and Arabs—in our own languages we hear them speaking about God's deeds of power." All were amazed and perplexed, saying to

one another, "What does this mean?" But others sneered and said, "They are filled with new wine."

But Peter, standing with the eleven, raised his voice and addressed them, "Men of Judea and all who live in Jerusalem, let this be known to you, and listen to what I say. Indeed, these are not drunk, as you suppose, for it is only nine o'clock in the morning. No, this is what was spoken through the prophet Joel:

'In the last days it will be, God declares,
    that I will pour out my Spirit upon all flesh,
        and your sons and your daughters shall prophesy,
        and your young men shall see visions,
            and your old men shall dream dreams.
Even upon my slaves, both men and women,
    in those days I will pour out my Spirit;
        and they shall prophesy.
And I will show portents in the heaven above
    and signs on the earth below,
        blood, and fire, and smoky mist.
The sun shall be turned to darkness
    and the moon to blood,
        before the coming of the Lord's great and glorious day.
Then everyone who calls on the name of the Lord shall be saved.'

"You that are Israelites, listen to what I have to say: Jesus of Nazareth, a man attested to you by God with deeds of power, wonders, and signs that God did through him among you, as you yourselves know—this man, handed over to you according to the definite plan and foreknowledge of God, you crucified and killed by the hands of those outside the law. But God raised him up, having freed him from death, because it was impossible for him to be held in its power. For David says concerning him,

'I saw the Lord always before me,
    for he is at my right hand so that I will not be shaken;
therefore my heart was glad, and my tongue rejoiced;
    moreover my flesh will live in hope.
For you will not abandon my soul to Hades,
    or let your Holy One experience corruption.
You have made known to me the ways of life;
    you will make me full of gladness with your presence.'

"Fellow Israelites, I may say to you confidently of our ancestor David that he both died and was buried, and his tomb is with us to this day. Since he was a prophet, he knew that God had sworn with an oath to him that he would put one of his descendants on his throne. Foreseeing this, David spoke of the resurrection of the Messiah, saying,

> 'He was not abandoned to Hades,
>   nor did his flesh experience corruption.'

This Jesus God raised up, and of that all of us are witnesses. Being therefore exalted at the right hand of God, and having received from the Father the promise of the Holy Spirit, he has poured out this that you both see and hear. For David did not ascend into the heavens, but he himself says,

> 'The Lord said to my Lord,
> "Sit at my right hand,
>   until I make your enemies your footstool."'

Therefore let the entire house of Israel know with certainty that God has made him both Lord and Messiah, this Jesus whom you crucified."

Now when they heard this, they were cut to the heart and said to Peter and to the other apostles, "Brothers, what should we do?" Peter said to them, "Repent, and be baptized every one of you in the name of Jesus Christ so that your sins may be forgiven; and you will receive the gift of the Holy Spirit. For the promise is for you, for your children, and for all who are far away, everyone whom the Lord our God calls to him." And he testified with many other arguments and exhorted them, saying, "Save yourselves from this corrupt generation." So those who welcomed his message were baptized, and that day about three thousand persons were added. They devoted themselves to the apostles' teaching and fellowship, to the breaking of bread and the prayers.

Awe came upon everyone, because many wonders and signs were being done by the apostles. All who believed were together and had all things in common; they would sell their possessions and goods and distribute the proceeds to all, as any had need. Day by day, as they spent much time together in the temple, they broke bread at home and ate their food with glad and generous hearts, praising God and having the goodwill of all the people. And day by day the Lord added to their number those who were being saved.

In *The Beginning of Difference*, Theodore Hiebert notes that Pentecost is "the church's charter."[2] That means it is a definition of what the church is and what the church is to become, whether we realize it or not. At Pentecost, the future was born in the eschatological Spirit in the present, a future of human community amid diversity. What follows is an attempt to re-member, put back together, theologically, this diverse human future and present that God has for the church and world, even in the face of their racialized fragmentation.

GIFT OF BREATH

A critical aspect of a pneumatology rooted in Pentecost is the notion of breath as a divine gift to all human beings. Note that even the coming of the Spirit on the day of Pentecost is a gift, that is, the result of divine intention and forethought. Jesus reminded the disciples of the "promise of the Father" and told them to wait for it (Acts 1:4). They had to wait to be baptized in the Spirit, because the descent of the Spirit is a gift, a bestowed promise, not something or someone of our own creation. "And suddenly from heaven there *came* a sound like the rush of a violent wind" (Acts 2:2). The sound came. The Spirit came on divine volition, reminding us that the Spirit is God's gift to us, to all people, all flesh, not limited to any one group. Divine agency is the prelude to human agency. Without God's breath, God's Spirit, there would be no human breath, no human life or action. This breath is what Howard Thurman calls "the givenness of God" that validates the worth of every human being.[3] This is true for all human creation, regardless of race, class, and gender. Breath, Spirit, is God's grand equalizer. That is, life and breath are a gift for all flesh, regardless of raced status. Life and breath are given by a giving God. Breath comes and it came, suddenly. If there was no sudden irruption of wind, breath, spirit, then there would be no disruption of the status quo

---

2. Theodore Hiebert, *The Beginning of Difference: Discovering Identity in God's Diverse World* (Nashville: Abingdon, 2019), 110.

3. Howard Thurman, "Black Pentecost #3: Footprints of the Disinherited," delivered during the Black Ecumenical Commission of Massachusetts meeting at Eliot Congregational Church, Roxbury, MA, May 30, 1972; http://archives.bu.edu/web/howard-thurman/virtual-listening-room/detail?id=360019.

monochromatic, univocal, homogeneous existence. But God's breath blows broadly and expansively across humanity and opens up the borders of human hearts toward each other. What we have at Pentecost is an "insurgency of the Spirit"[4] where a wind breathes on all people freely and generously.

If there is no breath, there is no life—as when a police officer choked Eric Garner to death as he said, "I can't breathe."[5] This is a practical, real-life example that demonstrates that if there is no breath, there is only death. Violence against racialized individuals is an expression of death, not the life of the Spirit. The breath of the Spirit, the wind of life, is a gift, a grace that should never be taken for granted. Gifts are given, not created by us, meaning all is gift. Grace cannot be racialized; it is extended by the Spirit to all humans. Therefore, no human group is self-made, nor is breath reserved solely for any particular human being. Breath is not raced or in a color; it is for all flesh and in all flesh. No human group can sustain itself without breath, the Spirit. We are gifted with breath, Spirit, and life that come as part of the givenness of God to all human beings.

This "natural" pneumatology is part of our common humanity, something with which we are all born: breath. An aspect of common ground is that we have a common breath. Ashon Crawley highlights how breath joins others when he writes, "Breathing is an ongoing openness to life that is always and exorbitantly social."[6] Breathing is a shared experience of the Spirit as we give and receive God's breath from one another and from all of creation. Acknowledging this gift of breath, the gift of the Spirit, the gift that is the Spirit, fosters a counterpoint to racial hierarchies, because breath cannot be racialized, nor can it be segregated for the privileged and powerful. Sons, daughters, young, old, and even the enslaved breathe from the Breath of God. In the Spirit, all can say, "We can breathe." All flesh is in-spirited. All have received gifts and life from the Spirit; thus all are called to be stewards

---

4. Willie James Jennings, *Acts: A Theological Commentary on the Bible* (Louisville, KY: Westminster John Knox, 2017), 2.

5. Joseph Goldstein and Nate Schweber, "Man's Death after Chokehold Raises Old Issue for the Police," *New York Times*, July 18, 2014, https://www.nytimes.com/2014/07/19/nyregion/staten -island-man-dies-after-he-is-put-in-chokehold-during-arrest.html?searchResultPosition=2.

6. Ashon Crawley, *Blackpentecostal Breath: The Aesthetics of Possibility* (New York: Fordham University Press, 2017), 48.

of breath. No race and no ethnicity are the life-givers, meaning that all human beings are life-receivers, even though at times humans aim to be life-takers. All that we have, including this one precious life on earth and the breath that makes it possible, has been received. All people, all flesh, are dependent on God. In this way, the Spirit of Pentecost is egalitarian, not hierarchical, in that all human beings have the same breath flowing in and through their bodies.

GIFT AND POWER TO SPEAK AND UNDERSTAND

The gift of breath in all is critical for this conversation on racialization, but so is the gift of power to witness, speak, and understand. The Spirit comes as a grace to all, but the Spirit also comes as power (*dynamis* in Greek, source of the English word "dynamite"). Before the day of Pentecost, Jesus tells the disciples, "But you will receive power when the Holy Spirit has come upon you; and you will be my witnesses in Jerusalem, in all Judea and Samaria, and to the ends of the earth" (Acts 1:8). Again, God's gracious action takes priority and propels human activity. In particular, the Spirit comes as power, a power to witness. The witness, however, is not constrained. Rather, the power to witness in the Spirit is a power to interact beyond oneself in order to expand racial-ethnic and cultural engagement across the typical racialized segregational silos. The Spirit's power is for an expansion in how we relate to and with diverse others such that our social borders are broadened into the vast vision of God. Without the reception of this power, there cannot be a move from racialization toward humanization, because it is the only means of living beyond who and what we know. The Spirit's power is what causes the movement toward the human other to the ends of the earth, with a hope to end dehumanizing racialization. It is not a human power but a holy one that reminds us of the source of everything good in the world, including transformative human relations.

It is also important to note that this power to witness is a power to die for this boundary-crossing engagement. "Witness" comes from the word "martyr" in this biblical setting, which is an indication that the reception of this power comes with great risks. Leaving one's known surroundings, relationships, and racialized group comes with the risk of death, at least a death to the way one used to live or to a certain mentality. The power of the Spirit, the *dynamis*, the dynamite of God, may blow up everything we thought we knew about other people or social races; thus this is a risky call. This power puts life as we know it in danger, but it does so for the future of God. To receive it is to be changed into more of whom the Spirit of Christ desires. It is a dynamite life, a powerful existence, perhaps one we always wanted deep down in our hearts. It is not a power to be played with, but rather to be pursued and prayed for, so that the Spirit might empower us to become more human.

This spiritual power not only reveals itself through an expansive witness but comes with a gift of speech. At Pentecost, we hear that "all of them were filled with the Holy Spirit and began to speak in other languages, as the Spirit gave them ability" (Acts 2:4). The Spirit enables humans to speak in other languages not even of their own culture. This speech is not human-made but in-spirited, in-breathed. It is "Spirit speech."[7] As Will Willimon writes, "The first gift of the Spirit is the gift of speech, the gift of speech in different languages."[8] What is most striking is how the Spirit enables multilingual speech. Those speaking with this gift are not speaking in their native language but the language of the *other*. The Spirit causes the mother tongues of those who are different to be on the tongues of the *other*. Their culture resides in the speech of those from another culture, creating a cross-cultural inhabitation. In the context of racialization, there has to be a willingness to learn the language of the raced other, with the recognition that although the language is different, it is still a human speech. At Pentecost, there is an integration of human beings through language in the Spirit, a gift of speech that comes with a purpose to be understood.

The gift of pneumatic speech is given in order that speakers may be understood, just as preachers preach in order to be heard and, they hope, understood. The gift of ecstatic speech at Pentecost is usually highlighted, but what is also stressed is how others *understand* what is being spoken. When the disciples are filled with the Spirit and speak in other languages as the Spirit enables them, "Jews from every nation under heaven" become bewildered and amazed because "each one heard them speaking in the native language of each" (Acts 2:5–6). The Spirit comes with the gift of understanding as well as the gift of speaking. The miracle is that they heard their native language out of the mouths

---

7. See Luke A. Powery, *Spirit Speech: Lament and Celebration in Preaching* (Nashville: Abingdon, 2009).

8. William H. Willimon, *Acts*, Interpretation (Atlanta: John Knox, 1988), 30.

of those from a different culture, yet they understood: "And how is it that we hear, each of us, in our own native language?" (Acts 2:8). This is why they have to ask, "Are not all these who are speaking Galileans?" (Acts 2:7). The speakers were not of the same ethnicity and culture, yet they understood even what the other spoke. The Spirit moves people toward understanding; "ecstasy is the catalyst for comprehensibility."[9] There is not just hearing or just speaking. At Pentecost, the Spirit stresses the dual gifts of speaking and understanding.

"Speaking the other's language" is important in conversations about race such that people do not speak *past* one another, but *to* one another in the hope of understanding and being understood. But the Spirit is the one who brings understanding. In Acts 2, although others may have heard, they did not always understand. Some were amazed at what was happening, "but others sneered and said, 'They are filled with new wine'" (Acts 2:13). Not all present on that day understood. Some mocked the cross-cultural communion, as some do in our time when it comes to race relations. Not all received the gift of the Spirit on that day to speak or understand, because it is only the Spirit that can foster the speech and understanding as manifested at Pentecost. This suggests that not every person will understand why moving through and beyond racialization toward humanization is vital for life in the Spirit and the future of the church in the world. Not everyone is receptive to this holy possibility and power, especially when it comes to race talk and the race walk. It may all seem romantic and unrealistic, as if one is drunk or in a dream. But if it is a dream, it is God's long and patient daydream in the Spirit for the flourishing of all people.

AFFIRMATION OF DIVERSITY

The egalitarianism of the Spirit's movement at Pentecost, particularly through the gift of breath or wind, is an implicit affirmation of the diversity of humanity, which confronts the dehumanization of racialization. This is perhaps why the observers in Acts thought the disciples were drunk: because the Spirit was poured out on *all* flesh, *all* bodies, not just a privileged few, which was the expected normative way of societal operation. The book of Acts emphasizes repeatedly how people were together, "all together" (Acts 2:1). But to be together in one place

9. John R. Levison, *Filled with the Spirit* (Grand Rapids: Eerdmans, 2009), 364.

does not mean that they were homogeneous in ethnicity or language. Not even the triune God within the Christian tradition is homogeneous, for God is three persons in one—Father, Son, and Holy Spirit. The miracle of Pentecost was that the people were different, particular, and yet remained together, showing us how the God of Pentecost is big enough to hold difference within the unity of the divine self. In the Spirit, difference is not a reason for demonization or dehumanization. Humans may not be able to hold such a wide stance, but God can. God is big enough through the "wideness of God's mercy,"[10] but what we have seen is that perhaps our theological constructions are not. They tend to be exclusive rather than more inclusive, racializing and segregating rather than more humanizing.

This turn to Acts and Pentecost in the Bible is one story of the beauty of human diversity. There are others,[11] all affirming the Bible itself as a diverse book. The Bible, as an authoritative source and guide in the church, is big enough to hold difference. This should be obvious due to its composition. It consists of different cultures, races, ethnicities, histories, times, places, and languages. It speaks in many voices, not just one; like Pentecost, it is polyvocal, polyphonic. The Bible is a pentecostal book in that multiple, diverse languages tell the story of God through the inspiration of the Spirit. Hiebert reminds us, "The Bible is essentially a library made up of a collection of writings composed over a thousand-year period in many different times and social contexts."[12] The Christian source book in its very composition values diversity and difference, despite the demonization and destruction with which racial difference has historically been met within the church. Yet within this larger biblical context of diversity, the story of Pentecost holds central importance.

As on the day of Pentecost, today some are amazed at the Bible's diversity, while others sneer at it or try to deny its existence. This pentecostal mix of culture, ethnicity, race, bodies, and language disturbs the usual relational, spiritual, and social sensibilities that keep "like" people together; this picture of diversity makes the onlookers at Pentecost think it is the last day of classes in a college semester, because they see what they think is a drunken frenzy in the morning. This scriptural

---

10. Frederick W. Faber, "There's a Wideness in God's Mercy," *The United Methodist Hymnal* (Nashville: United Methodist Publishing House, 1989), 121.

11. See the story of the Good Samaritan in Luke 10:25–37 and story of the eunuch in Acts 8:26–40.

12. Hiebert, *The Beginning of Difference*, xxiii.

image is fitting, because some people see diversity and difference as being drunk from sipping the libations of a secular ideology or political correctness. In truth, it is the gospel of God, a Pentecost ecology, a reflection of the beauty of God on earth or what Dr. King called the "world house."[13] Diversity is a gift of God, and Pentecost reveals that God embraces difference and does not erase who we are in our particularity. In fact, God creates humanity with all its difference, meaning that diversity is God-breathed. In the light of Pentecost, diversity or difference is the norm for the church, not a storm to be stilled. "Difference is God's work and God's intention,"[14] whether it be linguistic diversity, geographical diversity, or racial-ethnic diversity. The Spirit embraces diversity in all its forms. One might say that "the celebration of difference [is] a hallmark of Christianity."[15] Through the lens of Pentecost, there is no room for racialization and dehumanization. But there is much fertile space for the embrace of all human beings in their wide diversity.

Moreover, the miracle of Pentecost is that diversity and unity converge for a unified diversity. Difference does not mean division. All of them were filled with the Spirit and began to speak in different languages, but through different languages all spoke of God's deeds of power. Some think Pentecost or diversity is about divisiveness, but there can be genuine unity only if the members are diverse. Otherwise, there is only uniformity, not unity. This is why I coin the term "diversunity"—to indicate that there is no true unity without diversity. This is a way of reminding others that uniformity and unity are different realities, because there is no such reality as a diverse uniformity.

Nonetheless, despite being essential to unity, difference and diversity have been utilized to create splinters, divisions, and human hierarchies. Some can obsess over relatively small differences and use them to divide. Comedian Emo Philips makes this point very clear when he tells a story about a man who was going to jump off a bridge because he felt as if nobody loved him. Another person in conversation with this desperate man discovered that they both were Christian, Protestant, Baptist, and even of the "Northern Conservative Baptist Great Lakes Region." At that point, the man who wanted to jump was asked,

---

13. Martin Luther King Jr., *Where Do We Go from Here: Chaos or Community?* (1967; repr., Boston: Beacon, 2010), 177.

14. Hiebert, *The Beginning of Difference*, 120.

15. Hiebert, *The Beginning of Difference*, 139.

"Northern Conservative Baptist Great Lakes Region Council of 1879 or Northern Conservative Baptist Great Lakes Region Council of 1912?"

He said, "Northern Conservative Baptist Great Lakes Region Council of 1912." The other person said, "Die, heretic!" And [he] pushed him over.[16]

Uniformity means everyone looks the same, acts the same, thinks the same, and is the same kind of person. Uniformity really means that we are just worshiping ourselves and not a God whose beauty is embodied by multiplicity and diversity. The push toward uniformity, in regard to racialized identity or otherwise, implies that there is an operative norm or ideal that constitutes the imagined goal of a group. Any divergence from that norm is seen not as diversity, but as failure.

However, the day of Pentecost is not about uniformity. It is focused on the unity of a diverse people. As noted, there is a common idea that diversity, difference, or multiplicity means divisions and problems. But multiplicity or diversity is the context for unity in God. Diversity is what makes unity possible, because without multiplicity there will only be constant conformity. The gift of this Pentecost community, according to Michael Welker, is that it is "not a homogeneous unity, but a differentiated one."[17] Pentecost represents the preservation and goodness of human diversity, particularly as that applies to God's community. The Spirit does not dehumanize but embraces the particularities of every human being, including Black individuals who have been historically oppressed and dehumanized. The Spirit does not break us apart because of our differences, but rather pulls together a diverse human community of bodies and tongues. In this Spirit, the church is called to be unified, not uniform. A uniform church is no church at all, even though "advocates of congregational homogeneity . . . and others informed by the church growth movement have often argued that uniformity is a more realistic, expedient, and effective interim strategy prior to the eschaton."[18] The church is the church in the power of the Spirit when it is unified, a unified diversity focused on God. This is a powerful witness and countertestimony in a world that is divided and polarized around issues of race, racial difference, and racism.

16. Emo Philips, "The Best God Joke Ever—and It's Mine!," *The Guardian*, September 29, 2005, https://www.theguardian.com/stage/2005/sep/29/comedy.religion.

17. Michael Welker, *God the Spirit* (Minneapolis: Fortress, 1994), 228.

18. Lisa Lamb, *Blessed and Beautiful: Multiethnic Churches and the Preaching That Sustains Them* (Eugene, OR: Cascade, 2014), 43–44.

Eric Barreto argues that "human differences [are not] obstacles to unity to be transcended but theologically vibrant sites for God's action in the world."[19] Human differences and diversity are the critical variables that make unity possible and are sites for God's proclamation across the world. Diversity is not a problem but offers great potential for the future of proclamation "to the ends of the earth" (Acts 1:8). Pentecost reveals that "no single culture will corner the gospel message," and diverse cultures, languages, and ethnicities are "the authentic home of the gospel."[20] The gospel cannot be placed into a racialized hierarchy so that some people are excluded from speaking, hearing, or understanding the gospel. The gospel is for all and can come from all flesh in the power of the Spirit. This flesh is diverse and embodies human differences.

Sameness is actually more problematic than diversity, because diversity is a gift of God in the power of the Spirit, whereas sameness suggests humans are in charge. Yet we are born into an inescapable diversity where not even identical twins are exactly the same. When different people come together for work and witness, it is a sign that God is at work. If diversity is absent, we are likely only worshiping a god made in our own image, because there are people who cannot handle racial difference and will accept only their way, their race, their tongue, or their philosophy.

On a British Airways flight from Johannesburg, a middle-aged, well-off white South African woman found herself sitting next to a Black man. She called the cabin crew attendant over about her seating. "What seems to be the problem, madam?" asked the attendant. "Can't you see?" she said. "You've sat me next to a kaffir. I can't possibly sit next to this disgusting human. Find me another seat!" "Please calm down, madam," the stewardess replied. "The flight is very full today, but I'll tell you what I'll do. I'll go and check to see if we have any seats available in club or first class."

The woman gave a snooty look at the outraged Black man beside her (not to mention many of the surrounding passengers). A few minutes later the stewardess returned with the good news, which she delivered to the lady, who could not help but look at the people around her with a smug and self-satisfied grin. "Madam, unfortunately, as I suspected,

19. Eric Barreto, "Negotiating Difference: Theology and Ethnicity in the Acts of the Apostles," *Word & World* 31, no. 2 (2011): 131.

20. Hiebert, *The Beginning of Difference*, 140, 142.

economy is full. I've spoken to the cabin services director, and club is also full. However, we do have one seat in first class." Before the lady had a chance to answer, the stewardess continued, "It is most extraordinary to make this kind of upgrade, and I have had to get special permission from the captain. But, given the circumstances, the captain felt that it is outrageous that someone be forced to sit next to such an obnoxious person." With that, she turned to the Black man sitting next to the woman, and said, "So if you'd like to get your things, sir, I have your seat ready for you." At that point, many of the surrounding passengers stood and gave a standing ovation while the man walked up to the front of the plane.[21]

When we think of the Spirit of Pentecost and the formation of the church, it is not selfishly about "my way" or "my culture" or "my race" or "my tribe" or "my language" or "my personal biases," but God's way. God's way, then and now, includes "Parthians, Medes, Elamites, and residents of Mesopotamia, Judea and Cappadocia, Pontus and Asia, Phrygia and Pamphylia, Egypt and the parts of Libya belonging to Cyrene, and visitors from Rome, both Jews and proselytes, Cretans and Arabs" (Acts 2:9–11). God never erases human particularities— names, languages, cultures, ethnicities, skin color, hair texture, eye color, body shape, or other identifying markers. Therefore, we should never obliterate whom and what God has created, in order to suit our needs, comforts, opinions, and prejudices. God made all humans, and when we are tempted to erase that which is different, it is an affront to God and God's collective body. Pentecost is a revelation of how the Spirit works and speaks through every human's particularity as an avenue to real unity. Through the Spirit "I become more myself," not more like someone else. As Thurman teaches, each life in the hands of God is an authentic sacrament.[22] The Spirit, *pneuma*, hovers over human particularities and diversity as a gift of God.

Poet and priest Malcolm Guite writes that, on Pentecost, the Spirit's "mother-tongue is Love, in every nation."[23] God's way in the Spirit

---

21. This story is noted as a legend yet speaks to racial realities and can be used to combat racism. See David Mikkelson, "Obnoxious Airline Passengers," *Snopes*, March 3, 2001, https://www.snopes.com /fact-check/obnoxious-passengers/.

22. Howard Thurman, "Black Pentecost #2: Reflections on the Black Experience," delivered during the Black Ecumenical Commission of Massachusetts meeting at Eliot Congregational Church, Roxbury, MA, May 30, 1972; http://archives.bu.edu/web/howard-thurman/virtual-listening-room /detail?id=360484.

23. Malcolm Guite, "Pentecost," in *Sounding the Seasons: 70 Sonnets for the Christian Year* (Norwich, UK: Canterbury, 2012), 47.

enacts border crossings, not the construction of racialized walls of oppression and dehumanization. The way God builds the people of God in the Spirit is by diversifying humanity and expanding the circle of inclusion. The church becomes more whole, excellent, faithful, beautiful, unified, stronger, and more like God, the Spirit, when we diversify and are no longer locally clannish but global in scope. The irony is that we can unify only when we diversify, because there has to be diversity in order to speak of unity.

Many interpreters have viewed Pentecost as the inverse of the Tower of Babel scene in Genesis 11, where the divided tongues bring confusion and scatter the people, while at Pentecost divided languages bring understanding and gather the people in unity centered on God. God's vision for the church and the world is born in and through multilingual, multiethnic proclamation. In God's hands, the makeup of the church and the nature of the world are diverse. God's dream is "a house of prayer for all the nations" (Mark 11:17). This Pentecostal vision enabled William Seymour in the early twentieth century at the Azusa Street revival to state, "The color line was washed away in the blood."[24] He believed in the birth of a new creation that drew all races together in the Spirit. For him, a Black man in a racialized society, this was the real miracle, sign, and experience of Pentecost. The color line was erased, but this did not mean the loss of any individual's specific particularity as it contributed to the unified community.

GOD-CENTERED COMMUNITY

In the Spirit, this unified and diverse community centers on God, which is an important reminder for a theological exploration of race. The Spirit does make a turn to human particularity but also turns to God. The Spirit of God affirms all nations (*ethnē*) with their plethora of beautiful diversities and distinct idioms, while the common breath of God flows through all people. The particularity of each human being gives voice to the Spirit in their own tongues and bodies. Yet the cultural particularity of the Spirit's gift, as shown at Pentecost, is not contrary to the universal quality of proclamation, because we do not

---

24. As noted in William C. Turner, "Pneumatology: Contributions from African American Christian Thought to the Pentecostal Theological Task," in *Afro-Pentecostalism: Black Pentecostal and Charismatic Christianity in History and Culture*, ed. Amos Yong and Estrelda Y. Alexander (New York: New York University Press, 2011), 169–90.

proclaim ourselves (2 Cor. 4:5), including our racialized identity or any other aspect of who we are. There is, as Yves Congar writes, "the catholicity of witness."[25] At Pentecost, the Spirit blows on everyone—this is a universality—but the gift is that everyone does not relinquish their particularity; the gift is not only to experience the Spirit but to recognize the gift of one's own voice and language for a wider and worldwide proclamation and ministry.

The reception of divine breath and the gift of power to witness, speak, and understand are not the ends of proclamation but the means. They attest to the Real Gift. The people are ethnically different and speak in different languages, but they all speak of God's deeds of power. God is the underlying gift of Presence in this story. God is the universal common message of Spirit-filled proclamation, as the Spirit redeems our myopic and colonial inherited rhetoric of race. People heard in their native languages a message about God (Acts 2:11), not a sermon on "Seven Principles for Having a Happy Life" or a word that reifies the social construction of race.

A turn to the Spirit is a turn to God, not to race, even the human race. Pentecost privileges God as the universal content of proclamation through particular cultural means. The end is always God, but the means is always particular, holding together the creative relationship between particularity and universality. Both are gifts, yet God is central to pneumatic proclamation and ministry in the world. Dietrich Bonhoeffer once preached that people are bored with the church, and the cinema appears to be more interesting than the church, "because we talk too much about false, trivial human things and ideas in the church and too little about God."[26]

The Pentecostal Spirit will not allow us to forget about God, for, as Welker writes, "Through the pouring out of the Spirit, God effects a world-encompassing, multilingual, polyindividual testimony to Godself. In this way God attests to Godself in a process that unites people in a way that causes them both wonderment and fear."[27] Though there is a diverse community, there is unity around the presence of God, who created this community in the first place.

Howard Thurman tells of his visit with Gandhi in India, recounting

25. Yves Congar, *I Believe in the Holy Spirit*, trans. David Smith (New York: Crossroad, 1983), 44.

26. Dietrich Bonhoeffer, "Ambassadors for Christ," in *The Collected Sermons of Dietrich Bonhoeffer*, ed. Isabel Best (Minneapolis: Fortress, 2012), 90–91.

27. Welker, *God the Spirit*, 235.

how they sang the spiritual "Were You There?" As they sang, everyone bowed their heads, and then they said a prayer. Thurman said that moment "was drunk with the presence of God," which revealed to him that "God speaks with many tongues but with one voice."[28] At Pentecost, the one voice proclaims God within a diverse community in the power of the Spirit. Pentecost is a "community-building festival"[29] but it is a distinct community in which God is the center. Cultural and ethnic specificity is important, as noted already and named explicitly in Acts, but in the Spirit they are decentered though not erased or whitewashed; this is no color-blind pneumatology. The color line between human beings may be washed away in the Spirit, as Seymour believed, but color is not. God dethrones cultural or ethnic hegemony at Pentecost,[30] but cultural, ethnic, and racialized identities are not obliterated or torn into pieces either, as was done with Sam Hose. Diverse human, enfleshed bodies are fully present and fully inspirited, yet the Spirit leads proclaimers to speak about and praise God, not the distinct beautiful self.

At the same time, the gift of a word from God about God occurs within and creates a distinct and different community. The Spirit does not hide behind or promote God as a way to homogenize the human community. Though theocentric, Pentecost reveals the gift of a community that represents boundary-breaking realities across culture, ethnicity, race, and language. In the Spirit, there is no room for segregation or silos, because the Spirit works toward integration, collaboration, and mutuality to form a dialogical community. As Willie Jennings writes in his Acts commentary, "Where the Spirit of God is, there is divine desire not simply for God but for one another."[31] Through this communal interaction and proclamation, there can be greater understanding about each other as well as the fullness of God present in the world in the power of the Spirit.

The formation of a global community through the inbreaking of the Spirit breaks humanity out of its proclivity toward homogeneity and moves it to embrace a broad gospel for "the ends of the earth" (Acts

28. Thurman, "Black Pentecost #2."

29. Cheryl Johns, "Preaching Pentecost to the 'Nones,'" *Journal for Preachers* 36, no. 4 (Pentecost 2013): 7.

30. God dethrones tribalism at Pentecost, yet tribal gods still reign in society today. See the discussion in Frank A. Thomas, *The God of the Dangerous Sermon* (Nashville: Abingdon, 2021).

31. Jennings, *Acts*, 11.

1:8). The gift of God opens us toward a hospitable vision in which the Spirit is poured out on "all flesh" (Acts 2:17) for the future of proclamation across the world. Any culture or ethnic group anywhere can be a conduit of the Spirit; thus there is no limit to whom or where the gospel can be preached. Though a word may be contextual in a particular culture, the gospel is never enclosed or trapped within any culture. The gospel is free and open in the light of an expansive Pentecostal Spirit who knows no bounds, blows where she wills, and creates a diverse human community. Hiebert sums it up well:

> When the Holy Spirit embraces each culture as an authentic part of Christianity at Pentecost, God grants each culture equal worth. God recognizes no culture as the dominant or normative measure of Christian identity, not even the culture of Christianity's origins. God stigmatizes no culture's difference as deficient. And God excludes no culture from the church. Such an image of the church's radical pluralism guards against the fear and suspicion of difference. Such an absolute valuation of multiple ethnic identities counters the tensions, prejudice, and conflict that difference can provoke. The continuous translatability of the message makes difference the hallmark of the church.[32]

Pentecost suggests that the Spirit opens us up to the possibility of hospitable relationships across cultures and races, as opposed to closed systems and practices that restrain the full scope of the gospel message of God and human relationships. Pentecost challenges the church to refuse to homogenize its members in relation to words, deeds, theologies, preaching styles, biblical interpretations, dress codes, or other patterns, but rather to remember that the church is shaped into the beautiful diversity of God from its beginning to its end. Difference is critical to the identity of the church, and God is the one who declares that difference fruitful. This is what Pentecost reveals. The turn to the Spirit turns to God, but it is important to affirm that this turn to the Spirit is also a turn to real, particular human beings, bodies, and tongues. Pentecost is not a philosophical ideal but a physical reality and human experience, as pneumatology implies materiality and incarnationality, which is vital for earthly conversations about the rhetoric of race.

---

32. Hiebert, *The Beginning of Difference*, 142.

EMBRACE OF HUMAN BODIES

The ignited inner pneumatological experience at Pentecost reveals itself in outer pneumatological expression, because "a disembodied spirit is not the Holy Spirit."[33] God the Spirit desires enfleshment. The sudden, rushing, mighty wind or breath, blown in and through a people, takes on flesh, incarnates, through multiple ethnicities and languages. That which the critics on the day of Pentecost deemed drunkenness was ecstasy through pneumatology: ecstatic, embodied speech. That biblical scene represents what I call elsewhere a "holistic material pneumatology."[34] Thurman would refer to this as the "Spirit of God Without-Within."[35] The fiery Spirit manifests and is embodied, materializes, through real human flesh, diverse bodies. This is critical, in light of the aforementioned historical and biological racialized inhumanities against blackness in particular.

It is important to emphasize that the Spirit embraces Black flesh, Black tongues, Black bodies, and Black gifts. Blacks were the humans most often dehumanized through racialization, and the Spirit hugs them and all flesh with holiness, fire, and power in their particularity, and inspires all to breathe, speak, understand, and dance in joy within community. The Spirit humanizes by filling every human being and unleashing spiritual dynamite (*dynamis*) into every human life, that all might be baptized with breath and power. The Spirit is no respecter of persons but loves each person lavishly and pours out gifts unconditionally. The Spirit's embrace through this Pentecostal outpouring is vital for the historically dehumanized, those not embraced or loved as human beings, but seen as objects to be controlled and destroyed, as was done with Black bodies. In *Working the Spirit* Joseph Murphy writes, "The incarnated Spirit heals the split between who people really are, and who America has said they are."[36] The Spirit's favor and love poured out on each person at Pentecost affirm the value, worth, dignity, and humanity of each individual, regardless of race or ethnicity. This scene is a revelation of the Spirit's love for human bodies, a holy hospitality that resists demonization by filling and flowing through bodies. "This is no

---

33. Stanley Hauerwas and William H. Willimon, *The Holy Spirit* (Nashville: Abingdon, 2015), 46.

34. Powery, *Spirit Speech*, 2.

35. Howard Thurman, *The Centering Moment* (New York: Harper & Bros., 1969), 21.

36. Joseph M. Murphy, *Working the Spirit: Ceremonies of the African Diaspora* (Boston: Beacon, 1995), 175.

docetic love that shuns matter."[37] The beaten Black body is embraced as beautiful and a sign of the glory of God, indicating that embodied blackness matters. The colonizers might have called Blacks nonhuman or nonbeing, but the Spirit stamps each person as a human being full of Holy Spirit fire. Pentecost offers a positive theology for particularity and racialized difference, one that affirms blackness, brownness, otherness, and fleshiness overall. It is an implicit indictment of racialized strategies of dehumanization promoted by a perpetual anti-Black inhumanity. This sad history is anti-Spirit and anti-God, because assaults on human beings, of whatever race, are assaults on the glory of God in human flesh, all flesh.

Slavery, with its anti-Black dehumanization, was death-wielding, but the Spirit is life and humanizing. The Spirit initiates enfleshment as seen with the incarnation of God in Christ and inhabits human flesh, fills all human beings, empties gifts into all cultures, enacting a kind of "pneumatological kenosis."[38] Bodies are temples of the Spirit (1 Cor. 6:19), housing the divine presence within human flesh, revealing how God desires enfleshment and incarnation. "Divine desire is of the earth, of flesh and blood, body and dirt, of hunger and passion and eros,"[39] even bread and wine. This is so critical and humanizing for those whose physical bodies were disgraced by hanging and swinging from poplar trees.

Pentecost shows that the Spirit loves us so much that she wants to get inside of us, dwell in us, and commune with us in a bond of love. This divine outpouring is love for each person. The Spirit honors the bodies of all people—young, old, male, female, all human beings throughout the world. Pentecost is a fusion of the pneumatic, sonic, and somatic. These freed bodies are sites of the Spirit's work, fire, power, speech, and understanding, "site[s] of divine revelation,"[40] regardless of race, ethnicity, and gender. The Spirit is an equalizer and holy resister to racism and racial hierarchical systems.

That the Spirit fills all and rests on *all*, not just *some* bodies, is the affirmation needed in the face of historical dehumanization and provides an opportunity for those deemed nonhuman to reclaim their

---

37. Turner, "Pneumatology," 184.

38. See Nestor Medina, *Christianity, Empire, and the Spirit: (Re) Configuring Faith and the Cultural* (Leiden: Brill, 2018).

39. Jennings, *Acts*, 10.

40. M. Shawn Copeland, *Enfleshing Freedom: Body, Race, and Being* (Minneapolis: Fortress, 2010), 8.

humanity in God. Pentecost shows us that the spiritual is linked to the material, and thus that all human bodies matter to the life of faith. The glory of God is revealed through all human flesh and is "the sign of special favor from the spirit."[41] At Pentecost, each body and ethnicity is affirmed as sacred and of worth, a human being loved by God.

LOOSENING OF HUMAN TONGUES

The most evident human body part emphasized on the day of Pentecost is the tongue, because there is much speaking. But it is not "normal" human speech. It is tongues or *glossolalia*, which "is the speech of the undercommons . . . capacious and expansive, open and irreducible."[42] It is so expansive, open, and free that it is a surplus of new possibilities and new realities. A new thing is ignited, and no thing is left out. These open tongues of fire rested on each of those present, and all began to speak in other languages as the Spirit gave them ability. This is Spirit speech through which speakers proclaim in the native language of others who are surprised to hear their mother tongue from ethnic others.

This is amazing and perplexing at the same time, because tongues resist control and categorization. Tongues are free, blowing where the Spirit wills. They cannot be encased within a specific social race or people group, because the Spirit cannot be entombed, trapped, or enslaved. The new tongues—"God touching, taking hold of tongue and voice, mind, heart, and body"[43]—signify a holy carnival of new wine and a new way of being together in community. The inbreaking of the Spirit opens a new reality, new speech, new life, new community, and a new future. This fiery inbreaking sunders totalizing paradigms of sameness, whiteness, one tongue, one way, one thought, or one practice. The different languages are a spiritual surplus and reveal plurality as the working of the Spirit. Crawley writes, "To speak in glossolalic tongues is to believe in the plurality of experience itself, to perform and live into the otherwise."[44] A plurality of persons speak of God in diverse languages. The breaking out of excess tongues signifies the redemption of human bodies as vessels of the Spirit and breaks apart the racialization

41. Zora Neale Hurston, *The Sanctified Church* (Berkeley, CA: Turtle Island, 1983), 79.

42. Crawley, *Blackpentecostal Breath*, 242.

43. Jennings, *Acts*, 28.

44. Crawley, *Blackpentecostal Breath*, 241.

that leads to dehumanization. Fire falls and burns away illusions of any pure social race or people. Loosed tongues loosen the grip of those holding society captive through created, racialized hierarchies. These tongues set people free to be who God has called them to be, in all their diversity and beauty. Each person can speak only a language on their unique tongue, not some normative language from another tongue. It is as Thurman teaches: "The only life you have is your life and if you do not live your life, following the grain in your wood, being true to the secret which is your secret, then you must stretch yourself out of shape in order to hear the word."[45] At Pentecost, the Spirit ensures that each person can use *their* tongue, without the need to shape their culture, language, or race according to an invisible standard.

Furthermore, tongues of fire can break us into a new language about each other and break open a new discourse about God and a new creation, a new humanity. This break-dance of the Spirit at Pentecost through bodies decolonizes limiting, myopic, inhumane, racialized constructs, because each tongue unleashes "otherwise possibilities."[46] Tongues are an irruption that disrupts racial dominance and hierarchy and is an incarnate revelation of God's embrace of human flesh, all flesh, all tongues, as the lengthy list of nationalities and ethnicities present at Pentecost demonstrates. Something new is born on this day; as J. Kameron Carter writes, "To enter into Christ's flesh through the Holy Spirit's pentecostal overshadowing is to exit the gendered economy and protocols of modern racial reasoning."[47]

In the Spirit, we should exit racialization and enter a new economy, a new community, a new creation, a new race, the human race. New tongues break out for a new day in the Pentecostal life of God to revolutionize the current rhetoric of race in society. At Pentecost, something novel, never seen before, breaks loose into the world. It is a beginning that is a foretaste of an ending, a remaking of humanity in the power of the Spirit, because "the Holy Spirit is the humanizing Spirit" "fashioning and refashioning our humanity."[48]

This surplus of tongues represents an unspeaking, unlearning,

45. Thurman, "Black Pentecost #3."

46. Ashon Crawley, "Otherwise Moments," *The New Inquiry*, January 19, 2015, https://thenewinquiry.com/otherwise-movements/.

47. J. Kameron Carter, *Race: A Theological Account* (New York: Oxford University Press, 2008), 340.

48. Steven R. Guthrie, *Creator Spirit: The Holy Spirit and the Art of Becoming Human* (Grand Rapids: Baker Academic, 2011), 43.

unthinking, and undoing of a racialized control of human life. Tongues are a new way of speaking about God and one another, which is a hope of this book. Glossolalia are tongues of fire but also of power, dynamite, exploding hate speech for a new language of love and liberation. These tongues is free in the Spirit and will not be controlled by one colonial, dominant language. Mouths are free. Bodies are free. Humans are free. All flesh is free, not enslaved behind walls of inhumanity. Tongues are loosed when there is a fire in the Spirit, revealing otherwise movements of God in the world and the church.

TOWARD THE "WORLD HOUSE" OF GOD

Confronting racialization through the pneumatological lens of Pentecost opens up a different reality beyond racialization toward humanization, an inclusive vision for all of God's children with a common divine breath, yet diverse ethnicities, bodies, and tongues. It is a pneumatology for cosmology, a Spirit for the whole world, "to the ends of the earth" (Acts 1:8). This Spirit breaks boundaries and crosses borders of racialized hierarchies to move all into the expansive heart of a loving God. The center may be God, regardless of the particularities of the people's proclamation, but the Spirit blows centrifugally, never to be siloed, even within the divine self. The Spirit's *kenōsis* is always for a deeper communion with God and one another.

Breath flows in this community of "diversunity" to reveal the future present of God for God's people, all of God's people, all flesh. All human bodies are temples of the Spirit, and all tongues proclaim a speech of the Spirit. No human voice or body is denied the presence and fire of God. Humans, regardless of ethnicity or race, speak a multiplicity of languages to reveal the diversity of God from the beginning, which is the vision of the end. The multilingual tongues and multiethnic bodies at Pentecost reveal that the future present of God is the "great world house."[49] In what became his final book, *Where Do We Go from Here?*, Dr. King lays out his ultimate goal, his dream of dreams, the telos of his life's work, which he called "the world house." The term "world house" can also mean "beloved community" or "human family" or "new world order." Historian Lewis Baldwin notes that the "world house" refers

---

49. King, *Where Do We Go from Here?*, 167.

to "a totally integrated world, undeterred by human differences and committed to the ethical norms of love, justice, community, and peace. In more simplistic terms, 'world house' for King amounted to a global communitarian ethic that embraces persons across geographical and cultural boundaries."[50] In his theology King stressed *imago Dei*, the creation of all people in the image of God, alongside the reality of human interdependence. In his final chapter, on the world house, he writes:

> Every nation is an heir of a vast treasury of ideas and labor to which both the living and the dead of all nations have contributed. Whether we realize it or not, each of us lives eternally "in the red." We are everlasting debtors to known and unknown men and women. When we arise in the morning, we go into the bathroom where we reach for a sponge which is provided for us by a Pacific islander. We reach for soap that is created for us by a European. Then at the table we drink coffee which is provided for us by a South American, or tea by a Chinese or cocoa by a West African. Before we leave for our jobs we are already beholden to more than half of the world. In a real sense, all life is interrelated. The agony of the poor impoverishes the rich; the betterment of the poor enriches the rich. We are inevitably our brother's keeper because we are our brother's brother. Whatever affects one directly affects all indirectly.[51]

As King fought against racism and colonial racialization, he struggled in this way for all people and for justice for all. His goal was the world house, which he also called an ecumenical "worldwide fellowship that lifts neighborly concern beyond one's tribe, race, class, and nation . . . [as] a call for an all-embracing and unconditional love for all [people]."[52]

In this way, King was a Pentecostal in the best sense of the word, because the Pentecostal Spirit is for all people. Pentecost is the biblical precedent for the world house. It points to God's desire for the whole world. The dynamism of the Spirit offers a constructive way to approach racialized hierarchy and dominance, the history and biology of inhumanity—especially within the church. Pentecost is a constructive theological lens to confront racialized difference and dehumanization, providing "otherwise possibilities" for speaking about these issues.

50. Lewis Baldwin, "Foreword," in Hak Joon Lee, *The Great World House: Martin Luther King, Jr., and Global Ethics* (Cleveland: Pilgrim, 2011), viii.
51. King, *Where Do We Go from Here?*, 191.
52. King, *Where Do We Go from Here?*, 201.

Pentecost not only opens up a new speech and a new way of being in the multicolored world of God, but it creates a new world. It is a new creation ignited by the Spirit. The Spirit may be "unsought" or "unwanted" but is "intent on making all things new."[53] This includes new flesh, a new body for the people of God. All flesh makes up this new body, a new people, Jews and Gentiles. It is in fact a new race, a human race birthed by the Spirit of Christ. This world house of God is a human house for all people. This turn to the Spirit is a turn to the human, the human race, in resistance to colonial racialization and hierarchy toward God's vision and hope of humanization. Pentecost reveals this as all people speak of God in different tongues through different bodies. Christian spiritual renewal is not reserved for a few people or practices. This spiritual reality necessarily includes all people and all practices of proclamation. This turn to the human through a turn to the Spirit should then also turn, literally convert, the church's preaching and worship life today because the "history [of Pentecost] is now."[54]

53. Hauerwas and Willimon, *The Holy Spirit*, 35.
54. Jennings, *Acts*, 2.

4

There's Room for Many-a More

A Homiletic for Humanity

Get on board, little children, there's room for many-a mo'.

—Spiritual

My speech and my proclamation were not with plausible words of wisdom, but with a demonstration of the Spirit and of power. . . .

—1 Corinthians 2:4

The people project their humanity in the togetherness of the Spirit.

—James Cone[1]

INTRODUCTION

Sociologists tell us that racialized uniformity is the typical pattern of congregations in the United States. The church "favors racial homogeneity"[2] and promotes the historic racialized divides overall. In this way, one could say that the contemporary church does not exemplify Pentecost but, rather, is more like Babel, with one tongue grasping to gain and maintain power (Gen. 11). But Pentecost is now. The fire is not next time; it is now or never, when it comes to revolutionizing racialization in the church. History and biology perpetuated the otherness of blackness, but theology, and pneumatology in particular, provides another way and wind for blowing us in a more human and humane direction. The turn to the Spirit, as I have argued, turns us to the human, with all of our beautiful diversity, in resistance to the dehumanizing racialization of people. This theological turn should not only focus on ideas or philosophy, but make a difference in the practices of the church. It should be a practical pneumatology, hitting the ground where we walk and live through our breath, bodies, and tongues.

1. James Cone, "Sanctification, Liberation, and Black Worship," *Theology Today* 35, no. 2 (1978): 140.

2. Gerardo Marti, *Worship across the Racial Divide: Religious Music and the Multiracial Congregation* (New York: Oxford University Press, 2012), 15.

This chapter will show how the pneumatological turn to the human shapes some ecclesial theories and practices. In particular, it impacts worship, including preaching. Early church theologian Basil the Great once said, "If you remain outside the Spirit, you cannot worship at all."[3] This means you cannot preach at all. If there is no Spirit, there is no worship. If there is no Spirit, there is no word, as revealed through the gift of speech at Pentecost, reminding us of the *dynamis*, the dynamite, the power of words, even as made evident through the prophets of old. Life in the Spirit is broad, but because of the love of God "the route along which we travel the *spirit*ual life is neither that of blind mystery nor dogmatic knowledge, but of worship."[4] If worship, including preaching, is possible only in the Spirit, then one can understand the words of the apostle Paul: "My speech and my proclamation were not with plausible words of wisdom, but with a demonstration of the Spirit and of power" (1 Cor. 2:4). Because the Spirit's work on the day of Pentecost centers on speech, although there are numerous worship practices one can emphasize, I will narrow the focus to preaching and explore homiletics, the theory and practice of preaching. This exploration is not exhaustive, but suggestive of where the wind of the Spirit may be blowing related to worship in the church. If preaching is to be a "demonstration of the Spirit," a Spirit that moves through and beyond racialization to humanization, preaching too, in theory and practice, should be humanizing in its form, enfleshment, and message.

TYPICAL APPROACHES TO PREACHING AND RACE IN HOMILETICAL LITERATURE

Before delving into the rich implications of the Spirit for humanizing homiletics, we should first note that within homiletics there have been at least two approaches to the intersection of preaching and race. The first, and perhaps most obvious, is to focus on Black preaching and other racially minoritized preaching traditions written by racialized scholars.[5]

---

3. Basil the Great, *On the Holy Spirit* (orig. 375; Crestwood, NY: St. Vladimir's Seminary Press, 1980), 97.

4. Steven R. Guthrie, *Creator Spirit: The Holy Spirit and the Art of Becoming Human* (Grand Rapids: Baker, 2011), 15, italics mine.

5. See Andrew Wymer, "Betraying White Preaching: 'Responsible' and 'Realistic' White Preaching," The 2019 Academy of Homiletics Workgroup Papers (New Brunswick, NJ: Academy of Homiletics, 2019), 247–59.

I call this "raced literature." These scholars illuminate preaching traditions other than white as a way to offer distinctions and insights from
what has been considered normative. To be clear, HyeRan Kim-Cragg
notes, "Eurocentric philosophy, culture, and language have shaped the
place of preaching in North America. Despite the fact that there are
many preachers in North America today who do not conform to the
gender, race, and language of the colonial norm, the preaching place
today is still defined in terms of white male Anglo preachers."[6] According to Andrew Wymer, in their scholarship racialized and minoritized
scholars have tugged "at the masks of white preachers and white homileticians, forcing, at the very least, partial exposures of their 'faces.'"[7]
But he goes on to say that those efforts have basically been disregarded,
at least in the normative scholarship of the homiletics guild.

Nonetheless, these minoritized preaching traditions have set themselves apart and affirmed and recognized the beauty and distinctions
of their homiletical differences. There is a long tradition in homiletical scholarship centered on Black preaching through the work of such
individuals as Henry Mitchell, Cleo LaRue, Teresa Fry Brown, Marvin McMickle, Frank Thomas, Joseph Evans, Kenyatta Gilbert, and
Lisa Thompson.[8] In Latinx settings, the work of Justo and Catherine González and Pablo Jiménez have borne much fruit in the field
of homiletics.[9] Within Asian contexts broadly, Eunjoo Kim has been
a homiletics trailblazer.[10] These scholars reveal the contexts, traits,

6. HyeRan Kim-Cragg, *Postcolonial Preaching: Creating a Ripple Effect* (Lanham, MD: Lexington, 2021), 48.

7. Wymer, "Betraying White Preaching," 51.

8. See Henry H. Mitchell, *Black Preaching: The Recovery of a Powerful Art* (Nashville: Abingdon, 1990); Cleophus James LaRue, *The Heart of Black Preaching* (Louisville, KY: Westminster John Knox, 2000); Teresa L. Fry Brown, *Weary Throats and New Songs: Black Women Proclaiming God's Word* (Nashville: Abingdon, 2003); Marvin McMickle, *Preaching to the Black Middle Class: Words of Chal-lenge, Words of Hope* (Valley Forge, PA: Judson, 2000); Frank A. Thomas, *They Like to Never Quit Praisin' God: The Role of Celebration in Preaching*, rev. ed. (Cleveland: Pilgrim, 2013); Joseph Evans, *Reconciliation & Reparation: Preaching Economic Justice* (Valley Forge, PA: Judson, 2018); Kenyatta R. Gilbert, *The Journey and Promise of African American Preaching* (Minneapolis: Fortress, 2011); Lisa Thompson, *Ingenuity: Preaching as an Outsider* (Nashville: Abingdon, 2018).

9. See Justo L. González and Catherine G. González, *The Liberating Pulpit* (Eugene, OR: Wipf & Stock, 1994); Pablo A. Jiménez and Justo L. González, *Púlpito: An Introduction to Hispanic Preaching* (Nashville: Abingdon, 2005).

10. See Eunjoo Mary Kim, *Preaching the Presence of God: A Homiletic from an Asian American Perspective* (King of Prussia, PA: Judson, 1999); Eunjoo Mary Kim, *Women Preaching: Theology and Practice through the Ages* (Eugene, OR: Wipf & Stock, 2009); Eunjoo Mary Kim, *Preaching in an Age of Globalization* (Louisville, KY: Westminster John Knox, 2010).

power, contributions, and impact of nonwhite preaching traditions and how these preaching traditions have supported the surviving and thriving of those in their racialized communities. They aim to highlight minoritized communities in writing, because otherwise they would not be written into human existence as viable, meaningful, and worthwhile preaching traditions, at least in the guild. These scholars and others desire to be otherwise over against what has been the white norm in homiletics. They offer "otherwise possibilities" courageously and insightfully.

Yet there is another strand in homiletical literature for the intersection of preaching and race: having the actual sermon content focus on race and racism. In his book *How to Preach a Dangerous Sermon*, Frank Thomas claims that preachers do not often preach about issues of race, because they are explosive and can divide. Nonetheless, Thomas argues that if we do not "choose productive options and constructively confront issues of race and whiteness, the issues do not go away."[11] In a similar manner, Carolyn Helsel offers a courageous take on this topic in her book *Preaching about Racism*, as she speaks to white audiences and churches and offers strategies for preaching about racism. She writes, "If we are to recognize ourselves within the history and legacy of racism, we have to talk about how racism has impacted *all* people in society."[12] Helsel calls for conversation and respectful listening, while boldly naming the sin of racism as idolatry. Another book geared toward white churches is Will Willimon's *Who Lynched Willie Earle? Preaching to Confront Racism*. In this memoir-like work about a lynching in his native state of South Carolina and a local preacher's naming of it, Willimon argues that whites should first name their whiteness, as a way to claim being indoctrinated into racialized hierarchies. He, like Helsel, believes naming racism as sin is a means to recognizing the need for redemption. Both of these scholars take on this tough topic of racism and preaching, along with numerous minoritized scholars. We might refer to their approach as "preaching about racism" or "preaching against racism." These homiletical approaches join the "raced" preaching literature by minoritized homileticians already named.

These perspectives inhabiting the intersection of preaching and race can be expanded through another possibility, the pneumatological lens of Pentecost. Through the power, the *dynamis*, of the Spirit, there is a

---

11. Frank A. Thomas, *How to Preach a Dangerous Sermon* (Nashville: Abingdon, 2018), 35.
12. Carolyn Helsel, *Preaching about Racism: A Guide for Faith Leaders* (St. Louis: Chalice, 2018), 11.

homiletical approach that is more in line with "preaching *through and beyond* racism." It is an approach in the power of the Spirit that can turn homiletics to the human.

TOWARD A HUMAN (SERMON) FORM

What we need in the church and what I have been exploring is the essential presence and emergence of a new tongue and new creation in the Spirit to renew, reimagine, and even revolutionize our rhetoric of race. We need something, Someone, who transgresses space, time, and culture. We need pneumatic reasoning that emphasizes the human, and if preaching is "Spirit speech,"[13] then it should reflect the humanizing way of the Spirit in the flesh. There is a homiletical-theological "way to talk about difference, including racial difference, without granting our difference sovereignty."[14] As Pentecost reveals, God is the center, not any one human identity. We do not aim to make our identities idols. However, one must acknowledge honestly, as Matthew Kim does, that "ethnic minorities in American society on a consistent basis feel as though they need to fight for dignity, respect, and equality. . . . The default position is that the dominant culture gets its way because of their upper hand numerically and their concurrent hegemony."[15] Therefore, it is critical to talk about race and racialization without making the subject the sum total of the gospel and establishing our whole identity in racial particularity, because racial reasoning is insufficient for healthy gospel preaching and living a whole human life. Yet what is vital is Kim's observation about how minoritized people struggle for human dignity and respect. This can be because of how racialization has dehumanized real human beings in the past and present. Thus the church has an opportunity through homiletics, the theory and practice of preaching, to be a pathway for humanizing others.

When it comes to preaching, the Spirit reveals knowledge "through *human* proclamation of the Word."[16] In her stimulating work *The*

13. See Luke A. Powery, *Spirit Speech: Lament and Celebration in Preaching* (Nashville: Abingdon, 2009).

14. Will Willimon, *Who Lynched Willie Earle?: Preaching to Confront Racism* (Nashville: Abingdon, 2017), 66.

15. Matthew D. Kim, *Preaching with Cultural Intelligence: Understanding the People Who Hear Our Sermons* (Grand Rapids: Baker Academic, 2017), 103.

16. Aaron Edwards, *A Theology of Preaching and Dialectic: Scriptural Tension, Heraldic Proclamation, and Pneumatological Moment* (New York: Bloomsbury Academic, 2018), 163, italics mine.

Overshadowed Preacher, Jerusha Neal writes, "To understand Mary's pregnancy as a metaphor for sermonic action is to see both pregnancy and sermon as entirely human."[17] As we have seen, the Holy Spirit leads us into a "turn toward the human" in all its diversity. Homiletics in the Pentecost Spirit must move, more explicitly without reservation, beyond traditional thinking about sermon forms to include the human form.[18] Charles Campbell explores the scandal of the gospel through the lens of the grotesque, with all of its tensions and contradictions, as he challenges homiletics to be liberated from easy, closed-off answers, pulpit clichés, and false resolving patterns. In *The Scandal of the Gospel*, Campbell writes, "I wonder if the gospel and life really lend themselves neatly to many of our theological and homiletical patterns. . . . The grotesque . . . shocks us out of our comfortable patterns, including those many of us may rely on in the pulpit."[19] He also presses homileticians and others to confront the dehumanizing powers that loom in the world. In particular, he calls for resistance to the weaponizing of the grotesque that dehumanizes blackness and other *others*. Again, he presents a "word before the powers"[20] in the power of the Spirit.

For my purposes, what is illuminating in Campbell's work on the scandal of the gospel is the way the carnival of a Pentecostal God enfleshed in a grotesque Christ explodes typical conversations and perspectives about sermon form in homiletics. Through the Spirit, though pneumatology is not an emphasis for Campbell in his work, there is an affirmation of the grotesque, which is an affirmation of all people, that is, the incarnate human form, rather than traditional neat and tidy sermon forms. In the Spirit, we turn to the sermon form of human flesh, bodies, and tongues, with the recognition that a pneumatology in, of, and for preaching is an expansion, an explosion, a broadening, not a narrowing, through which the Spirit blows sermon forms to include the human form. For example, this might mean placing a primary emphasis in a preaching course on the person of the preacher as it relates to character, spiritual formation, cultural rootedness, and embodiment,

---

17. Jerusha Matsen Neal, *The Overshadowed Preacher: Mary, the Spirit, and the Labor of Proclamation* (Grand Rapids: Eerdmans, 2020), 127.

18. For a traditional understanding of sermon forms or patterns, see Ronald J. Allen, *Patterns of Preaching: A Sermon Sampler* (St. Louis: Chalice, 1998).

19. Charles L. Campbell, *The Scandal of the Gospel: Preaching and the Grotesque* (Louisville, KY: Westminster John Knox, 2021), 3, 5.

20. See Charles L. Campbell, *The Word before the Powers: An Ethic of Preaching* (Louisville, KY: Westminster John Knox, 2002).

prior to any instruction on biblical exegesis or other technical matters; it is a reorientation of homiletical pedagogy and its priorities toward the human. In this way, a pneumatology in, of, and for preaching expands the notion of sermon form such that the human form is a homiletical form, a per-*form*-ance, an enfleshment. How can it not be so when the Word became human flesh through the ushering of the Spirit in the tabernacle of the earth?

A turn to the human form through pneumatological reasoning resists dehumanization and the "thingification" of racialized human beings; it affirms all humans as beautiful creatures of God. The Spirit challenges homiletics to become more humanizing, that is, more compassionate, empathetic, and loving, bearing fruit of the Spirit, especially toward the other, even toward creation as a whole. A homiletic for humanity embodies reverence for all of creation while enacting what Howard Thurman calls the "reverence for personality"[21] toward human beings, nurturing the sanctification of humankind. The emphasis is on people over patterns, and more attention is given to the human form as a sermon form, rather than the typical pedagogical understanding of sermon forms and methods. How could this not be the case when the theological foundation for all of Christian preaching is rooted in Jesus Christ, who, though he was in the form of God, took on the form of a slave and, being found in human form, humbled himself to the point of death on a cross (Phil. 2:6–8)?

Homiletical alignment with the Spirit is an alignment with the human form of Christ, the foundation for all proclamation. Notice that the explosion of tongues at Pentecost in Acts is followed by Peter's sermon, which focuses on the person of "Jesus of Nazareth, a man" (Acts 2:22). "In Acts it is the person of Christ that matters, the embodied Jesus, crucified, raised, and reigning."[22] Again, the Spirit leads to the human and, in this case, to the person of Jesus Christ. What a human form, indeed! If we take the Christ hymn of Philippians 2 seriously and hold to the belief that the incarnation is an act of the Spirit, then what is demonstrated is how the performance of God, God's enfleshed sermon, is human, a human form, even the form of a slave. Jesus as the incarnation of God is "God's self performance,"[23] "the flesh and blood,

---

21. Howard Thurman, *Jesus and the Disinherited* (Boston: Beacon, 1949), 104.
22. Neal, *The Overshadowed Preacher*, 79.
23. Charles L. Bartow, *God's Human Speech: A Practical Theology of Proclamation* (Grand Rapids: Eerdmans, 1997), 26–27.

aural-oral, face-to-face speech event of divine self-disclosure."[24] When
God spoke God's Word, when God performed, it was in the flesh of a
human voice and body. God's self-disclosure was a performative event
embodied in the flesh: a human form.

Primary to a pneumatological lens in homiletics is the human form,
not a racialized one that is dehumanized. Before teaching on the various typical sermon patterns in classrooms, for this project on the rhetoric of race, it is vital to emphasize the human form, rooted in the form
of a slave, that led to the death of Jesus. Of course, like Peter's sermon
in Acts, Philippians paints the picture of resurrection and ascension as
well, but again, it is the human form of God in Christ that is emphasized. This should not be surprising, because the way of the Spirit, even
in preaching, is a human way.

Moreover, in relation to this conversation on race, it is a challenge to
all homileticians, and really to all people, to recognize that the form of a
slave is a human form, not a nonhuman one, as colonial powers taught.
Through a Christ-slave, God chose to show love and what it means to
love through the human form, specifically the form of a slave. This is
radical, revolutionary love and should challenge who we think is truly
human. In the Spirit, a slave saves; the racialized redeems and ushers in
a renaissance to the ends of the earth. As J. Kameron Carter writes, "In
taking on the form of the slave, the form of despised dark . . . flesh there
is the disclosure of divinity, a disclosure that undoes the social arrange-
ment of the colonial-racial tyranny."[25] This is an irruption of the Spirit
amid corruption, even within the church, to call us to humanize the
undervalued and underside of society.

In the Spirit, homiletics is pressed toward the human form above
all else. Homiletical matters are human matters. Humans cannot hide
behind traditional sermon forms, because the human form is the primary homiletical form. For example, preachers should stop asking God
to "move me out of the way," because the Spirit's way in preaching is
a human way. This means a preacher's prayer should be: "Lord, make
me fully present as myself. Make this an incarnational moment. Ignite
my own idiom." The Spirit nudges us to embrace our whole human
selves in public, not to fade away or be erased, even in the face of acts
of dehumanization. Preaching is sacramental, and the cost of such a

---

24. Bartow, *God's Human Speech*, 36–37.
25. J. Kameron Carter, *Race: A Theological Account* (Oxford: Oxford University Press, 2008), 342.

performance "is being exposed as human."[26] The human form as hom-iletical form in the Spirit means that even racialized slaves prophesy, and the dehumanized have their humanity hugged by God as conduits of the gospel.

HUMAN ENFLESHMENT OF THE WORD

As human form in the Spirit, there is a necessary affirmation of enfleshment, incarnation, of human breath, bodies, and tongues, a liberating gesture especially for those who have been dehumanized by colonial racialization. To borrow the words from one of my favorite "unchurched" preachers, Baby Suggs, holy, in Toni Morrison's *Beloved*, there is "flesh that needs to be loved."[27] The unleashing of the Spirit's power into human beings, into preachers, as at Pentecost, moves hom-iletics closer to human flesh in its theories and practices. For some, this approach may look like drunkenness, when it is really an expression of holiness on earth, when God touches the human through breath, voice, and bodies. This is a homiletic pneumatology of intimacy that can invite the church and world to become more fully human with God.

Stewarding Breath

To speak of the intimacy of enfleshment leads to the nearness of the Spirit in human breath. To be human is to breathe, to receive breath from Holy Breath, and to love this breath, because without it there is only death, spiritual and physical. A homiletic for humanity acknowl-edges the necessity of receiving breath. It affirms that breath is vital to preaching. Physiologically, breath is the power of the voice, the power of the spoken word. Without breath, there can be no words spo-ken. Breath is even more important than books, even the Holy Book, because the Holy Breath antecedes the formation of the Bible (Gen. 1:2, 30). When the Spirit, the breath of God, comes at creation or the new creation at Pentecost, she breathes into creatures, not books, into human beings from all over the world. When Evans Crawford talks about "the hum" of preaching and the "pause" in sermons, he argues

---

26. Neal, *The Overshadowed Preacher*, 134.
27. Toni Morrison, *Beloved* (1987; repr., New York: Vintage, 2004), 104.

that it is "an opening in the preacher's consciousness through which the musicality of the Spirit breathes, so that the musicality of the sermon resonates with the living truth."[28] During the COVID-19 global pandemic, we have seen the damage and death that come from a virus that strikes the respiratory systems of human beings where people cannot breathe. Breath is a divine gift, so a human emphasis in homiletics means that there is no room for proclaimers to say, "I can't breathe," because the "Spirit is life" (Rom. 8:6). Preaching is a breathing room, making space for all people to breathe. In that way, preachers are stewards of breath, divine and human.

This aligns with what James Forbes writes: "The preaching event itself—without reference to specific texts and themes—is a living, *breathing*, flesh-and-blood expression of the theology of the Holy Spirit."[29] The Spirit breathes into preachers as recipients, but then preachers also release this breath into the world. Preachers do not steal breath from others but, rather, share it with them. Like in Ezekiel and the valley of dry bones, preachers in the Spirit proclaim with God, "You shall live" (Ezek. 37:5–6), in order that others can testify, "I can breathe." In order to release this breath, preachers should engage in *epiclesis*, an invocation for the Spirit to come. What the prophet Ezekiel does in the valley of dry bones, we should also do: "prophesy to the breath" (Ezek. 37:9). Preachers ask the Spirit to come so that they may blow her breath into the church. This is breath that needs to be loved and nurtured, filling voices, bodies, and congregations. It is human to breathe, and this is foundational for a humanizing homiletic—a deep yearning that all may breathe and never die. This release of breath is a release from the history of lynching, which robbed one of breath, chaining it and choking it. Preaching is the release of breath in the freedom of the Spirit within a community. Ideally, preaching releases others, especially racialized individuals, to be free in tongues and bodies as anti-lynching homiletical performances.

This pneumatic freedom of breath is clearly evident in the whooping tradition of the Black church. "Whooping is the intentioned apportioning of breathing, the making of breathing stylistic, the making audible the flow of air into and out of lungs. The whooping moment incites the congregation to ecstasy, heightens the intensity of emotion,

---

28. Evans E. Crawford and Thomas H. Troeger, *The Hum: Call and Response in African American Preaching* (Nashville: Abingdon, 1995), 17.

29. James A. Forbes, *The Holy Spirit & Preaching* (Nashville: Abingdon, 1989), 19, italics mine.

is the solicitation to which congregants respond with energy and conviction."[30] This musical celebration in preaching known as whooping is individual but also communal. In whooping, there is often a call and response, a homiletic of antiphony, or a collective breath, in and out, receiving and releasing. Breathing as humans is deeply communal, and the Spirit, the Holy Breath, "is grounded in the necessity for sociality. Not only does Spirit give life, but that life is evident in how one leans toward others, how one engages with others in the world. We do not merely share in sociality; we share in the materiality of that which quickens flesh; we share air, breath, breathing through the process of inhalation and exhalation."[31]

Voicing Meaning

Just as the Spirit, the breath, is the power of the word throughout the Scriptures, human breath is the power of the human voice, a vocation of sounding meaning. A pneumatic homiletic is sonic, resonating with the human voice. Breath supports the vocation of voice, a spirituality of meaning-making through sound. When we discuss *pneuma*, sound is associated with it. Even at Pentecost in Acts 2:2, "there came a sound like the rush of a violent wind." Even when Mary, the soon-to-be mother of Jesus, was overshadowed by the Spirit and greeted her cousin, Elizabeth, we learn that "when Elizabeth *heard* Mary's greeting, the child leaped in her womb. And Elizabeth was filled with the Holy Spirit" (Luke 1:41). A certain sound may signify or usher in the Spirit; in these cases, one is from the natural world, but the other is from a human voice like Mary's. This intersection of Spirit, sound, and voice suggests what Greg Goodale argues: "The voice is the pneuma, which means both 'breath' and 'spirit' or 'soul' in a manner that gives life to communication. The voice moves; the voice occupies space. Even when captured, the voice is never static. The voice, then, marks one's identity better than the body."[32] The human voice is free like flowing breath, even if the body is confined; the Black creators of the spirituals understood this. In addition, as voice is linked to vocation (from Latin

---

30. Ashon Crawley, *Blackpentecostal Breath: The Aesthetics of Possibility* (New York: Fordham University Press, 2017), 43.

31. Crawley, *Blackpentecostal Breath*, 40.

32. Greg Goodale, "The Race of Sound," in *Sonic Persuasion: Reading Sound in the Recorded Age* (Champaign: University of Illinois Press, 2011), 95.

vocare, "to call"), "the voice is the person," whoever they may be, and "it is prototypically human."[33] To be human is to have a voice, even if others try to mute one's voice.

The homiletical voice, therefore, is human and is an instrument of the Spirit in the ministry of proclamation. As humans are distinct, so are the voices, so are the sounds that make meaning. James Weldon Johnson wrote about how the voice of early Black preachers was like a trombone,[34] but for others, their vocal instrumentations may be more like a violin, cello, or clarinet. A human turn via a turn to the Spirit is an acknowledgment of the varied homiletical sounds possible in pulpits. No voice is subpar in the Spirit; voices and vocations differ, but that difference does not have to lead to dehumanization. A humanizing homiletic nurtures all human voices, all identities, because the wind, the breath of the Spirit, blows through multiplicity and polyphony. Just as Chimamanda Ngozi Adichie teaches about "The Danger of a Single Story,"[35] there is the danger of a single sound or single meaning when it comes to preaching. Human voices are diverse in their texture because of the gift of the Spirit, not despite the Spirit. If racialized voices and sounds are shut down, this is anti-Spirit, aiming to choke breath out of humanity through the inhumane tactics of oppression.

Homileticians ought to be mindful of how the racialization of sound and particular voices have been treated in the wider culture, so that they do not perpetuate this form of dehumanization in classrooms and in churches. For instance, there has been a distinction made between noise and sound in broader society; blackness is associated with noise, which is a problem in the context of ongoing colonialism. During the early-twentieth-century Pentecostal revivals on Azusa Street, police were called in because of the noise that was disturbing the peace. "To rid the area of such noise would have rid the area of the flesh—black, white, indigenous, Mexican, Korean—that gathered together at 312 Azusa Street for their revival."[36] Certain sounds were racialized, and thus policed. There is a "sonic color line" that persists in our time.

---

33. Goodale, "The Race of Sound," 97.

34. See James Weldon Johnson, *God's Trombones: Seven Negro Sermons in Verse* (New York: Viking, 1927).

35. See Chimamanda Ngozi Adichie, "The Danger of a Single Story," filmed July 2009 in Oxford, UK, during TEDGlobal 2009; TED video, 18:33, https://www.ted.com/talks/chimamanda _ngozi_adichie_the_danger_of_a_single_story?language=en.

36. Crawley, *Blackpentecostal Breath*, 145. For further insight about noise versus sound, see his entire chapter on "Noise," 139–96.

"Whiteness . . . is notorious for representing itself as 'invisible'—or in this case, inaudible (at least to white people). The inaudibility of whiteness stems from its considerably wider palette of representation and the belief that white representations stand in for 'people' in general, rather than 'white people' in particular."[37] The sonic division perpetuated by colonialists and the promoters of racialization distinguish noise from sound, and loud from quiet, with the latter being acceptable while the former is despised. "Racialized sonic politics" can form a racialized sonic homiletic. This is dangerous and deadly for preaching, which aims to be the voice of God to the people of God. Attunement to this dynamic recognizes the danger that certain voices or people will be thought to represent God, while others will not. In particular, history reveals that "whites represent[ed] black people as the least sonically categorizable as human, let alone as potential citizens."[38]

A human approach in homiletics realizes the necessity to resist this racialized perpetual history through the affirmation of a multiplicity of voices and sounds. Acoustemology, the experience of sound as a way of knowing, is not only theology, but sociology as well. The sounds of voices send messages about who is in and out in the church and the world. Refusal to allow diverse homiletical vocal music in pulpits reveals the belief that particular identities are an aberration, because standing in a pulpit is the affirmation of a voice, a vocation. Homiletical "music is a potent bearer . . . of ethnic memory, identity, and station";[39] a rejection of certain music in the pulpit tells people they are not welcome. This often happens to Black women and others, revealing that sound is also gendered, not just raced. Lisa Thompson, in her book *Ingenuity*, remembers when an elder church mother told her, "I don't like women preachers. But I like you. You don't sound like a man, but you don't sound like a woman either."[40]

I understand this complex issue of voicing meaning through sound as a human in a pulpit. Hearers are socialized into listening patterns

---

37. Jennifer Lynn Stoever, *The Sonic Color Line: Race and the Cultural Politics of Listening* (New York: NYU Press, 2016), 12. One example she gives is that "[w]hen middle-aged white man Michael Dunn murdered seventeen-year-old [Jordan] Davis at a Florida gas station in 2012, . . . he marked his aural territory. Dunn didn't want to hear hip-hop at the pumps, so he walked to the jeep where Davis and his friends were listening to music and demanded they turn it down. When the teenagers refused, Dunn shot into their car and fled." For this story, see p. 2.

38. Stoever, *The Sonic Color Line*, 33.

39. James R. Nieman and Thomas G. Rogers, *Preaching to Every Pew: Cross-Cultural Strategies* (Minneapolis: Fortress, 2001), 51.

40. Lisa Thompson, *Ingenuity: Preaching as an Outsider* (Nashville: Abingdon, 2018), 3.

and into what is deemed noise and what is deemed sound. When I started at Duke Chapel, I received many questions; one was, "Why do you sing when you preach?" There are many reasons for singing the gospel in the pulpit, but for me, singing in preaching has been an aspect of my own voice and vocation, as well as critical to my cultural and ecclesial ancestry. Behind that question, sometimes, was an expectation of a single monolithic sound, or even a certain identity, in the pulpit. But through my voice and body, something new was emerging in a more consistent manner than usual in this university chapel setting. This acoustical difference signified racial, cultural, denominational, and theological difference—because even sound is raced. Yet in the Spirit, "[s]inging the gospel in the pulpit is not a race or denominational thing. It is a human thing, a life and death thing."[41]

Preaching is a human phenomenon in the Spirit, not a racialized one, such that when we hear distinct sounds in the pulpit, it is a human sound of the Spirit, not a "Black sound" or a "white sound." This is vital to the embrace of the Spirit of all human beings who stand behind the sacred desk. However, let me add to this conversation on voice and sound the importance of what is actually said and meant from human voices through human sounds in Christian pulpits. It is critical to remember that the Spirit not only provides power for the physical mechanism of the human voice and sound, but the Spirit is also the one who affects what one actually proclaims. What a preacher says from the pulpit and in daily life also matters. In the Spirit, the meaning flowing from a homiletical voice should be life-affirming, not death-wielding, as was the case with colonial master-preachers. The Spirit will inspire words of praise, hope, truth, lament, forgiveness, liberation, love, and all of the fruit of the Spirit, as opposed to curses, lies, hate, or gossip (1 Cor. 13; Gal. 5:22–23; Eph. 4:29–32). Preaching in the Spirit has the ultimate aim of always building up the people, never tearing them down, because the manifestation of the Spirit in preaching is "for the common good" (1 Cor. 12:7).

The human voice is a sound of the Spirit, but there should always be a spirit of discernment about the meaning of certain sounds, because even discernment is a gift of the Spirit (1 Cor. 12:10). This word of caution does not prohibit or limit the deep spiritual connection of the voice as noted in Eastern Orthodox settings and others where singing is emphasized. In that setting,

---

41. Luke A. Powery, "Singing the Gospel in the Pulpit," *Divinity Magazine* (Spring 2016): 13.

prolonged, disciplined breathing—which is what singing is very much about—potentially effects communion with God's Holy Breath in a manner that we moderns, possibly owing to a kind of Gnostic, Docetic, or even crypto-Manichean pneumatology usually overlook. Imagine the sacramental power of acknowledging and enacting one's inhalation and exhalation as a means of communing with the Spirit.[42]

All breathe, thus all commune with the Spirit, consciously or unconsciously. There is no sound without breath, no vocalization without inhalation and exhalation.

The potential of communing with the Spirit through breathing, voicing, singing, is a truly unexplored gift to humanity. This communion can also shape a deeper union between others, as the gift of breath and voice in the Spirit can bring others into their own sound and voice. This is what happened with Naomi and Gladys. Naomi was a Jewish woman and Gladys an elderly, fragile African American woman with Alzheimer's, unable to speak. Naomi became vulnerable and humble and sang Christian songs to Gladys as a way to reach her, because she knew Gladys grew up with these songs in church. One day, Naomi rubbed Gladys' right arm up and down, stared into her eyes, and then began to sing, "Jesus loves me, this I know." As Naomi continued to sing, Gladys began to keep tempo with her right hand. When that song was finished, Naomi rubbed both of Gladys' cheeks with her hands as she began to sing, "He's got the whole world in his hands." Something amazing happened when Naomi started to sing the verse, "He's got the mothers and the fathers in his hands." Naomi sang, "He's got the mothers and the fathers," and Gladys, who could not speak, responded antiphonally, "in his hands." After the singing stopped, Naomi, with her hands on Gladys' cheeks, asked Gladys, "You feel safe? With Jesus?" Gladys in a soft whisper responded, "Yeah."[43] This is a holy communion in the Spirit, face to face, breath to breath, voice to voice, song to song, human to human. This is what is possible in and out of pulpits when Breath breathes in and through our voices.

42. Peter Galadza, "The Holy Spirit in Eastern Orthodox Worship: Historical Enfleshments and Contemporary Queries," in *The Spirit in Worship—Worship in the Spirit*, ed. Teresa Berger and Bryan D. Spinks (Collegeville, MN: Liturgical, 2009), 135–36.

43. For this story, see "Gladys Wilson and Naomi Feil," May 26, 2009, https://www.youtube.com /watch?v=CrZXz10FcVM.

Loving Bodies

Furthermore, to be human is to have not only breath and a voice, but a body. Thomas Troeger gives an apt definition of homiletics as "theology processed through the body."[44] Body is not a metaphor in this case, as in some of the apostle Paul's writings (e.g., 1 Cor. 12:12–31). It is material reality. Lisa Thompson argues, "Preaching is carried out by flesh and lands upon flesh. Therefore, we cannot discard the body as a vehicle, nor its influence, in carrying forth the memory of preaching in a community."[45] Homiletics is such a human enterprise that fleshy, even crucified, bodies are at its heart. The flesh that needs to be loved are those who have been hated historically, denied access to pulpits all over the world because of a designated race, class, or gender. A homiletic for humanity resists the brutalization of racialized bodies and embraces them as divine, beautiful, and blessed. This humanizing homiletic blesses blackness and otherness and implicitly intones the spiritual, "There's room for many-a mo'." What happened to Black farm laborer Sam Hose is the result of dehumanizing theologies and practices, but pneumatology can redeem Black bodies, not from physical death, but from the "wiles" of inhumane enemies, social death, and destructive theology. Homiletics can hug the dehumanized in order to humanize, which is the way of the Spirit.

In Morrison's *Beloved*, Baby Suggs, holy—despite having "busted her legs, back, head, eyes, hands, kidneys, womb and tongue" through the grind of slavery—declares a message to the gathered collective Black body present in the Clearing. From her "heart," she tells them to love their flesh, "love it hard," because "[y]onder they do not love [their] flesh." Eyes, skin, hands, face, mouth, feet, backs, shoulders, arms, neck, liver, heart, lungs, and womb are parts of the "flesh that needs to be loved." Her bodily message is not only explicit but also implicit, as revealed in the sermonic climax, when "[s]aying no more, she stood up then and danced with her twisted hip the rest of what her heart had to say."[46] Her body was preaching without even saying a word. This performance signified her love for Black flesh. This scene is known as a "liturgy of the Spirit"[47] which shows that the site of the Spirit is the site

---

44. Thomas H. Troeger, "Emerging New Standards in the Evaluation of Effective Preaching," *Worship* 64, no. 4 (1990): 294.

45. Thompson, *Ingenuity*, 25.

46. Morrison, *Beloved*, 102–4.

47. M. Shawn Copeland, *Enfleshing Freedom: Body, Race, and Being* (Minneapolis: Fortress, 2010).

of the human body. The Spirit loves Black bodies and other racialized bodies and all bodies in fact. But it is dark bodies that have experienced the brunt of inhumane brutalization.

Spirit possession of Black bodies has been an important reclamation of Black humanity within Black religion overall. But even with this understanding of pneumatic ecstasy, Black women and their bodies have been a site of extreme interrogation. "We live in a world that has violently contested the presence of black women's voices and bodies."[48] The scholarship of Teresa Fry Brown highlights this injustice. In *Weary Throats and New Songs*, she details the challenges that Black women have faced in the church as preachers and pastors.[49] Her book title itself is a metaphor for their experience. She uses "weary throats" to describe their weariness from ongoing resistance to their calling, yet speaks of "new songs" because of their resilience and hope in the face of opposition to continue to proclaim the music of the gospel in the Spirit. To be clear, her literary language is more than metaphor. It is material, because physical bodies of Black women have been mistreated and unjustly interrogated, even though their bodies, too, are temples of the Spirit who affirms their humanity. The new song will be sung because the Spirit cannot be stopped. Black bodies will praise and preach, swing and sway, when the wind blows on and through them. This is glory divine, flesh divine, humanity divine.

The presence and process of loving bodies, all bodies, Black bodies, gendered bodies, as a humanizing gesture in homiletics "creates new visions for both the image of preacher and the image of justice."[50] Although we have inherited a history of racialized inhumanities, this does not mean that this is the future of preaching in the church. In the Spirit, something new is created and born in and through human flesh. Breath pulsates through bodies and tongues. In particular, when Henry Mitchell and others stress using vernacular language, a native tongue, in preaching, he calls this the "mother tongue of the Spirit,"[51] because it is particular and enfleshed in such a way that others hear their own tongue and idiom as the Spirit translates a word through and to multiple languages and bodies. The word comes through mother tongues

---

48. Thompson, *Ingenuity*, 15.

49. Teresa Fry Brown, *Weary Throats and New Songs: Black Women Proclaiming God's Word* (Nashville: Abingdon, 2003).

50. Thompson, *Ingenuity*, 19.

51. Henry H. Mitchell, *Black Preaching: The Recovery of a Powerful Art* (Nashville: Abingdon, 1990), 76–87.

because the Spirit speaks through diverse ethnicities and roots born from a mother's distinct womb of flesh.

All of this love shown to bodies through the Spirit of love is the human work of the divine Spirit. It is a work of healing, resistance, and redemption. When speaking about Black preaching traditions, Dale Andrews writes, "Preaching participates in the formation of Black wholeness which is nothing short of re-humanizing Black personality."[52] Making the wounded whole through a whole embrace of the broken Black body in particular as resistance to racialization is a gesture of re-humanization in the Spirit. Loving bodies that have been dehumanized is how the Spirit rehumanizes those who have been cast out of humanity by the inhumane.

This loving gesture has rich potential for re-membering homiletics, and helps us understand that, while homiletics is closely tied to the Bible, it is the body, and not the Bible itself, that preaches. A human homiletic emphasizes the human performing preacher as *homo performans*. The body talks and it speaks and knows things and God differently than other ways of speaking and knowing.[53] Loving bodies helps homiletics become more holistic and more pneumatological. In the Spirit, preachers think with "the bowels and brains."[54] Bodies are the *milieu d'esprit* as the Spirit honors the human body and makes it holy. It is important to remember that within the Christian tradition, "the sacraments state that the word of God wants to enter our bodies, that is, our lives, and that for anyone in-dwelt by the Spirit the road of the God of Jesus Christ necessarily uses the human road."[55] Homiletics should remain on this human road so that human beings become more

52. Dale Andrews, "Black Preaching Praxis," in *Black Church Studies: An Introduction*, ed. Carol B. Duncan, Juan Marcial Floyd-Thomas, and Stacey M. Floyd-Thomas (Nashville: Abingdon, 2007), 211.

53. See Mark L. Knapp and Judith A. Hall, *Nonverbal Communication in Human Interaction* (Australia: Wadsworth Thomson Learning, 2002), and Howard E. Gardner, *Frames of Mind: The Theory of Multiple Intelligences*, 10th ed. (New York: Basic, 1993).

54. This is what Charles Bartow said in a conversation with me in the fall 2006. The work of Mark Johnson supports this perspective. In *The Body in the Mind: The Bodily Basis of Meaning, Imagination, Reason* (Chicago: University of Chicago Press, 1990), he argues that all rational engagement with the world has its roots in our gestures, motions, and bodily experiences. See pp. 74–75.

55. Louis-Marie Chauvet, *The Sacraments: The Word of God at the Mercy of the Body* (Collegeville, MN: Liturgical, 2001), 114. For more insightful conversations about the theological value of the body, see Stephanie Paulsell, *Honoring the Body: Meditations on a Christian Practice* (San Francisco: Jossey-Bass, 2002); *Bodies of Worship: Explorations in Theory and Practice*, ed. Bruce Morrill (Collegeville, MN: Liturgical, 1999); and Kimberly Long, *The Worshipping Body: The Art of Leading Worship* (Louisville, KY: Westminster John Knox, 2009).

fully human, more embodied, more loving toward their flesh, as they engage in *homilētikos* under the aegis of the Spirit. Preachers should get in touch with their ordinary flesh—the same flesh, the same form, in which God entered the world in order to love. The human horizon shifts homiletics beyond "textocentrism"[56] to the enfleshed word, a human word known in the human flesh of Jesus Christ.

HUMAN MESSAGE

Preaching Jesus

Like James Weldon Johnson's *God's Trombones*, in some sense, preachers empowered by the Spirit will implicitly proclaim the words of this spiritual, "You may have all dis world but give me Jesus."[57] The Spirit points to Jesus, even in homiletics, but especially for a humanizing homiletic. I say this because even Peter's sermon in Acts, what has been viewed as the first Christian sermon, "begins only after the Spirit has come."[58] His christocentric sermon flows out of the wind of the Spirit. Notice that the Spirit does not move people to proclaim the Spirit. The Spirit moves people to proclaim what God has done in Christ, the story of Jesus. Peter says, "Listen to what I have to say: Jesus of Nazareth, . . . this man, handed over to you according to the definite plan and foreknowledge of God, you crucified and killed by the hands of those outside the law. But God raised him up, having freed him from death, because it was impossible for him to be held in its power" (Acts 2:22–24). "Moralism [in preaching] is a poor substitute for the death and resurrection of Jesus."[59] Christ's story, Christ's life, is the theological core for a pneumatic turn in a homiletic for humanity. Peter focused on "Jesus of Nazareth . . . this man," the person, the human, the one in flesh. His sermonic story does point to how Jesus is more than human in that he is "exalted at the right hand of God . . . [and] with certainty that God has made him both Lord and Messiah" (Acts 2:33–36), yet

---

56. Dwight Conquergood, "Performance Studies: Interventions and Radical Research," *Theater and Drama Review* 46, no. 2 (2002): 151.

57. Johnson, *God's Trombones*, 2.

58. Willie Jennings, *Acts: A Theological Commentary on the Bible* (Louisville, KY: Westminster John Knox, 2017), 34.

59. Willimon, *Who Lynched Willie Earle?*, 68.

he reminds hearers of Jesus' place and rootedness in Nazareth. In the Spirit, Jesus has central place in preaching. Jared Alcántara, drawing on Miroslav Volf, suggests that "Jesus-Christ-as-center" is primary for proclamation.[60]

Jesus stands at the heart of this humanizing homiletic. The preeminent subject of sermons—even if not explicitly and literally named in every single sermon—is Jesus. The Spirit blows preachers in his direction. The Spirit may create a community or establish the church (as some argue took place at Pentecost), but the Spirit leads people to proclaim "God's deeds of power" (Acts 2:11), not the church. "Jesus of Nazareth" is the one we proclaim in the Spirit, the one we are called to follow on the way. At times there is ecclesial confusion when people are more interested in following the church than Jesus. This is a dangerous anti-Spirit approach, because sometimes to follow Jesus one has to resist the church, especially when it comes to racism and racialization. Even within an academic field like homiletics, there is no substitute for a "Christological word."[61] All of the theories and practices of deconstruction, even deconstruction of our conceptions of Jesus, should ultimately lead back to Jesus as the center of preaching; this is what a pneumatological emphasis does. For instance, the spiritual homiletical tradition reveals how "in the Spirit, the past, present, and future of Jesus are the homiletical hub of hope."[62]

It is Jesus who is the Anointed One, the Messiah, which means he is anointed by the Holy Spirit.[63] In Trinitarian theology, the Holy Spirit is the Spirit of Christ; therefore to discuss the Spirit in preaching necessarily points to Jesus. William Turner, when discussing pneumatology and Pentecostals, writes, "Calling the name of Jesus amounted to an invocation of the Spirit. The sense was that Jesus is the pneumatic Christ."[64] Within this framework, it is unsurprising that Jesus is central

---

60. Jared E. Alcántara, *Crossover Preaching: Intercultural-Improvisational Homiletics in Conversation with Gardner C. Taylor*, Strategic Initiatives in Evangelical Theology (Downers Grove, IL: IVP Academic, 2015), 123.

61. Sally A. Brown and Luke A. Powery, *Ways of the Word: Learning to Preach for Your Time and Place* (Minneapolis: Fortress, 2016), 31–32.

62. Luke A. Powery, *Dem Dry Bones: Preaching, Death, and Hope* (Minneapolis: Fortress, 2012), 85–86.

63. For more on the anointing of Jesus, see Forbes, *The Holy Spirit & Preaching*, 41–52.

64. William C. Turner, "Pneumatology: Contributions from African American Christian Thought to the Pentecostal Theological Task," in *Afro-Pentecostalism: Black Pentecostal and Charismatic Christianity in History and Culture*, ed. Amos Yong and Estrelda Y. Alexander (New York: New York University Press, 2011), 171.

in a pneumatic homiletical emphasis. Jesus, "full of the Holy Spirit" (Luke 4:1), is even the one who begins what some call a sermon with, "The Spirit of the Lord is upon me, because he has anointed me" (Luke 4:18). Likewise, the Spirit on Peter at Pentecost propels him to preach Jesus.

This Jesus, however, is presented as human, grounded in the earth upon which all feet have trod. Peter seems to emphasize "this Jesus whom you crucified" (Acts 2:36). He is Lord and Messiah, and yet he is the crucified one. He is divine but surely human. Though he is raised and seated at the right hand of God, we remember how human he was, especially in that he was oppressed and crucified—a critical perspective for those who have been racialized and dehumanized. Like the apostle Paul, Peter knows nothing "except Jesus Christ, and him crucified" (1 Cor. 2:2). This moves a homiletic for humanity to attend to the plight of wounded people: the pain and suffering, the brokenness, and beaten, bruised bodies of crucified peoples all over the world. Preaching Jesus in the Spirit involves not just the triumph of the resurrection but the terror of the crucifixion, where God revealed his humanity most starkly.

Lament in Preaching

A pneumatological turn in homiletics to Jesus, particularly his cruciform nature, reminds us of how the Spirit leads Jesus to a wilderness and the prophet Ezekiel to a valley of dry bones, that is, to places of struggle, doubt, suffering, and death. The Spirit groans with all of creation, and so homiletics should groan too. In other words, our preaching should lament.[65] If preaching is an act of worship, it is important to remember that "worship evoked by the Spirit [is] from the place where the world is in pain."[66] For homiletics to be for humanity, it has to take seriously the historical and contemporary context of crucifixions, such as the experiences of racism and enslavement of Black peoples. Lisa Thompson argues, "If we do not privilege the lives and truth of the most vulnerable in our communities, then we cannot be faithful to the most fundamental work of preaching itself."[67] In the Spirit, preaching

---

65. For more about the groaning of the Spirit and a link to the work of Christ, see Luke A. Powery, *Spirit Speech: Lament and Celebration in Preaching* (Nashville: Abingdon, 2009), 24–31.

66. Teresa Berger and Bryan D. Spinks, *The Spirit in Worship—Worship in the Spirit* (Collegeville, MN: Liturgical, 2009), 22.

67. Thompson, *Ingenuity*, 7.

is a human task and much of humanity, even a human Christ, suffers tremendously. This should not be ignored if one is a human preacher, nor should one strive to avoid the truth of human reality, especially racialization, because "those who avoid pain and struggle will not bring forth life in the pulpit."[68]

Homiletics must pay attention to life's pain, but also offer constructive responses to it. One key homiletical response to human suffering is lament.[69] Preachers in the Spirit should name the sin of racialization but then also lament it publicly without fear. This "blues sensibility"[70] in preaching requires courage, as there may be opposition. But if we do not confront the issue of racism, it will only grow its tentacles of harm. Thus, we lament, even as we observe how pain does not go away. Racialization does not disappear. Resurrections do not erase crucifixions, as blood continues to spill across our world. Thus, a constructive homiletical approach for resisting racialization is to nurture unashamedly the voice of lamentation in preaching. Lament is direct speech and calls out injustice and the human suffering that it has caused, in the hope that God will do something about it through divine and human means. According to Kenyatta Gilbert, a prophetic word, which is often lament, "to communities in crisis . . . is a Word of life in the place of death—a daring dispatch of hope in the predicament of human suffering."[71] Prophetic lament tells the truth and works to exorcize the powers of dehumanization in any form for the flourishing of all people.

Preachers lament for the good of the whole, for a larger vision of what it means to be God's people on earth, to suffer with those who suffer and mourn with those who mourn. Lament can emphasize the individual, but it is also deeply communal in nature, because it knows that all humans are bound together by the Spirit's breath, tears, and love. "As people of faith, we are all called to attend to the suffering of one another,"[72] which is what lament does. It allows us to sit with each other in the ashes and in the valleys, and from that place speak up and out into the ear of God. Preachers should strive to identify with those suffering in their midst. More specifically, "it is in the purview of every

---

68. Forbes, *The Holy Spirit & Preaching*, 86.

69. For more on lament in preaching theory and practice, see Powery, *Spirit Speech*.

70. See Otis Moss III, *Blue Note Preaching in a Post-Soul World: Finding Hope in an Age of Despair* (Louisville, KY: Westminster John Knox, 2015).

71. Kenyatta R. Gilbert, *A Pursued Justice: Black Preaching from the Great Migration to Civil Rights* (Waco, TX: Baylor University Press, 2016), 132.

72. Helsel, *Preaching about Racism*, 4.

culturally intelligent preacher to unmask and sympathize with our listeners who have experienced deep-seated wounds as minority group members and to provide avenues for authentic healing and reconciliation, especially with injuries from the dominant culture."[73] Lament affirms the worth of the wounded. More importantly, it points to and fosters a sense of "shared suffering in the face of horror."[74] Even more than the performance of call-and-response in the preaching moment, this nurturing of shared suffering in community can be viewed as an "ethics of antiphony,"[75] meaning a responsive alternation of mutual care as a communal ethic. This ethic of the Spirit ultimately nudges the human community toward reconciliation.

Preaching toward Reconciliation

In our time, the term "reconciliation" has lost much of its meaning through overuse and has been cheapened by the omission of truth-telling and justice. Nonetheless, as Christians, we have a "ministry of reconciliation" (2 Cor. 5:18). This includes preaching. As Richard Lischer writes, "The end of preaching is reconciliation."[76] If racialization is, as one scholar notes, an "estrangement,"[77] then the emphasis in a humanizing homiletic in the Spirit should be on coming together as God's diverse children. The Spirit is "the Spirit of fellowship,"[78] of *koinōnia*; thus, a humanizing homiletic will stress reconciliation, because this is who God is in Christ. A homiletic for humanity understands that this move toward reconciliation is the "ultimate gospel gesture,"[79] as it emphasizes the hope of a beloved human community in God. There are biblical and theological underpinnings for "intercultural proficiency"[80] and inclusiveness and for such a reconciliatory

---

73. Kim, *Preaching with Cultural Intelligence*, 106.

74. Andrews, "Black Preaching Praxis," 207.

75. Paul Gilroy, *The Black Atlantic: Modernity and Double Consciousness* (Cambridge, MA: Harvard University Press, 1993), 79.

76. Richard Lischer, *The End of Words: The Language of Reconciliation in a Culture of Violence* (Grand Rapids: Eerdmans, 2005), 133. For a fruitful and substantive conversation on reconciliation, see Allan Boesak and Curtiss Paul DeYoung, *Radical Reconciliation: Beyond Political Pietism and Christian Quietism* (Maryknoll, NY: Orbis, 2012).

77. Helsel, *Preaching about Racism*, 76.

78. For more about this perspective homiletically, see Powery, *Spirit Speech*, 77–90.

79. Lischer, *End of Words*, 153.

80. Alcántara, *Crossover Preaching*, 120.

message, where the dividing wall of hostility is torn down in Christ (Eph. 2). Even more needed is the reminder of our common humanity that is broken and blessed.

It is important to remember that in the context of this conversation about reconciliation, we are talking about human beings, real people, flesh and blood and breath—not ideas, objects, or theologies. The message of reconciliation in the Spirit is human to human, and this includes race to race. Matthew Kim astutely points out this reality when discussing ethnic minorities. He writes, "We do not want to always commence the relationship with Others by talking about ethnic and cultural differences. Begin by acknowledging them as people."[81] People are first people, not an ethnicity or a social race. This is perhaps foundational through a pneumatological lens and is an affirmation of the theological concept of the *imago Dei*.[82] A humanizing homiletic has a core proclamation that stretches all the way back to Howard Thurman's grandmother, who heard the reassuring message from enslaved preachers: "You are a child of God!"[83] One preaches the humanity of all to all human beings, regardless of racialized status.

Underneath this proclamation is a deep sense of mutual humanity. Without this, there can be no real reconciliation. Even within the purview of Afrocentric orality, "The desired nature of speech is the expression or pursuit of harmony that can only be experienced with the restoration of the self, and that cannot be separated from community."[84] The restoration of the self, and especially the Black self that has been historically and perpetually dehumanized, is key for the whole of human reconciliation; but alone, it is insufficient for the entire vision of harmony. Harmony, reconciliation, is sought, rooted in a communal sensibility. Black preaching praxis has even been described "as an event in community."[85] Beyond the traditional call-and-response performed in Black preaching traditions, Evans Crawford states that "call and response [is] an expression of life in Christ."[86] It is an expression of the anointing in preaching. All people, all human beings, are a part of this antiphonal reality, because all are children of God.

---

81. Kim, *Preaching with Cultural Intelligence*, 112.
82. Matthew Kim speaks to this in *Preaching with Cultural Intelligence*, 104.
83. Thurman, *Jesus and the Disinherited*, 49.
84. Andrews, "Black Preaching Praxis," 208.
85. Andrews, "Black Preaching Praxis," 212.
86. Crawford and Troeger, *The Hum*, 55–56.

When the Spirit preaches toward reconciliation, there is also a sense that, as Eunjoo Kim teaches, "the context for preaching is the entire world."[87] If that is the case, preaching is ecumenical, coming from *oik-oumenē*, meaning the whole "inhabited world." The diverse world is the context of preaching, and so is the diverse church as reflected at Pentecost. Therefore, preaching that is honest about its macro context will not endorse a racialized mentality or attempt to essentialize any one socially constructed race. Every person within a particular racialized group is distinct because human beings, even within a so-called racial group, are not homogeneous. For any given sermon, there are multiple hearers and learners; thus, to preach toward reconciliation also means to widen one's homiletical arsenal, as well as "broadening the base of preachers."[88] This will stretch preachers and an entire church community to recognize that reconciliation entails being uncomfortable at times, to speak and hear different tongues and see different bodies.

Con-text—literally meaning "with text"—for preaching is everything that is "with" the biblical text; this includes all of the components, experiences, and practices of a preacher's entire life at home, work, church, recreation, in their community, and in the world, that inform and shape the entire sermon-making process from preparation to delivery. For this conversation on preaching toward reconciliation, con-text raises the issue about how people are embodying reconciliation around the practice of preaching, that is, what resources and sources they are using in sermon preparation. For instance, this indicates the status of where a community is going as it relates to reconciliation. Is it ecumenical in the fullest sense of the word?

The movement toward reconciliation suggests that "the preacher needs to have a cosmopolitan personality."[89] This is a personality that is sensitive and knowledgeable of the world, the whole cosmos. The Spirit moves preachers to the ends of the earth and broadens perspectives, widens eyes, and tunes ears to various tongues. Gardner Taylor was known to possess "improvisational intercultural proficiency." In an interview Taylor describes those "who have escaped the boundaries of habitation, who are able to address people with the gospel that

---

87. Eunjoo Mary Kim, *Preaching in an Age of Globalization* (Louisville, KY: Westminster John Knox, 2010), 19.

88. Lisa Washington Lamb, *Blessed and Beautiful: Multiethnic Churches and the Preaching That Sustains Them* (Eugene, OR: Cascade, 2014), 175.

89. Kim, *Preaching in an Age of Globalization*, 108.

does not belong to an ethnic dimension."[90] Taylor understood how the Spirit pressed preachers beyond their confines to embrace the entire cosmos. He was fluid throughout his ministry, because he flowed in the Spirit across racialized boundaries. He could not be limited, because he did not limit what was possible with God, the God of all humans. As James Forbes writes, "The god-of-race makes us run away from people and feel safer in the confines of sameness."[91] For Taylor and others who preached toward reconciliation, the God of humans makes us run toward each other.

Although this homiletic for humanity encourages the ministry of reconciliation now, true reconciliation between racialized groups is really an eschatological reality and challenge. There may be glimpses of God's reconciliation, but theological honesty will say that it has not been consummated.[92] All of the struggles in society reveal that reconciliation has not totally transpired. However, when churches embody *koinōnia*, the fellowship of the Spirit, the church is "a concrete witness to and an anticipatory presence of God's coming reign."[93] Brian Blount calls multicultural worship "the apocalypse of worship, the realization of its end-time, multicultural reality."[94] Like Pentecost, reconciliation is a present and future sign of the kingdom of God, a foretaste of the end of human history. Preaching toward reconciliation is a gesture that points to a time and world that is not yet fully present, and is a hope for the beloved human community in the presence of God. Preachers in the Spirit envision a future for human beings where all flourish and where all are one in Christ. HyeRan Kim-Cragg's conception of postcolonial preaching attempts to "move beyond naming the broken reality and offers a glimpse of the imagined world, the world as God

90. Alcántara, *Crossover Preaching*, 124.

91. James A. Forbes Jr., *Whose Gospel? A Concise Guide to Progressive Protestantism* (New York: The New Press, 2010), 84.

92. An important historical manifestation of the hard work of reconciliation in the world was South Africa's Truth and Reconciliation Commission in the wake of the struggle against apartheid. For an account of this work, see Desmond Tutu, *No Future without Forgiveness* (New York: Doubleday, 1999). For a more recent expression of the work and struggle toward reconciliation in light of the racial violence experienced at Mother Emanuel AME Church in Charleston, SC, on June 17, 2015, see Stephanie Hunt, "Mother Emanuel Five Years Later," https://faithandleadership.com /mother-emanuel-five-years-later.

93. Kim, *Preaching in an Age of Globalization*, 53.

94. Brian K. Blount, "The Apocalypse of Worship: A House of Prayer for ALL the Nations," in *Making Room at the Table: An Invitation to Multicultural Worship*, ed. Brian K. Blount and Leonora Tubbs Tisdale (Louisville, KY: Westminster John Knox, 2001), 27.

intends it to be. This is an important aspect of rehearsal in preaching."[95] In the Spirit, preachers rehearse reconciliation until it comes, because it is what is truly needed in a racialized world that divides and dehumanizes. This homiletical rehearsal not only speaks of how God makes creation whole, but proclaims a God who "reconciles us into a new humanity."[96] This new humanity through the work of the Spirit shapes more than preaching; it influences all of ministry, such that one may speak of doing ministry with humanity.

95. Kim-Cragg, *Postcolonial Preaching*, 7.

96. Kim-Cragg, *Postcolonial Preaching*, 7. For further reflection on a robust reconciliation, see J. Deotis Roberts, *Liberation and Reconciliation: A Black Theology*, 2nd ed. (Louisville, KY: Westminster John Knox, 2005). Howard Thurman too offers fruitful insights into reconciliation in his *Disciplines of the Spirit*, 5th ed. (Richmond, IN: Friends United, 1997), 104–27.

5

There Is a Balm

A Ministry with Humanity

There is a balm in Gilead to make the wounded whole.

—Spiritual

In the beginning was the Word. . . . And the Word became flesh and lived among us.

—John 1:1, 14

The story of Jesus of Nazareth [is] the paradigm of humanization.

—Eunjoo Kim[1]

INTRODUCTION

The work of the Spirit is helpful in opening up new and fresh ways to confront racialization and to begin to put the church on a constructive path as it relates to human relations. Pentecost is God's future-present promise for the church and its engagement with racialized difference. Yet the honest words of Howard Thurman remind us that "the Christian institution has been powerless in the presence of the color bar in society. . . . It has reflected the presence of the color bar within its own institutional life" and has not responded to the "genius of the Gospel which it proclaims."[2] Rather, the church has been a "tragic witness"[3] to the gospel. According to Thurman, this has occurred because the church "is not wide open to the Spirit of the living God."[4] Openness to the Spirit should open us to new ways of being, thinking, and doing in the world as it relates to the history of racialized inhumanity. Openness to the Spirit should also open us up to one another as fellow human beings, not racialized objects, because through the Spirit, it is possible to move through and beyond racialization toward humanization.

---

1. Eunjoo Kim, *Preaching in an Age of Globalization* (Louisville, KY: Westminster John Knox, 2010), 58.

2. Howard Thurman, *The Luminous Darkness: A Personal Interpretation of the Anatomy of Segregation and the Ground of Hope* (New York: Harper & Row, 1965), 105, 107.

3. Thurman, *Luminous Darkness*, 107.

4. Thurman, *Luminous Darkness*, 107.

In the Spirit, every person is an incarnate gift of God. This impacts homiletics, for example, as already discussed, but it also implicates ministry in general, the focus of this chapter. There is a homiletic for humanity through a pneumatological lens, but there is also a ministry with humanity that can be a healing balm in the Spirit for the world's divisions. After engaging the thought of Thurman on the human as a useful intellectual partner for this understanding of ministry, four key components of ministry with humanity will be explored: following Jesus, attending to suffering bodies, striving for community, and embracing mortality. In the Spirit of Pentecost, this ministry approach is resistance to the powers of racialization for the renewal of humanization. Some have called it a "revolution."[5] I call it a revival, a renaissance, a rebirth of our humanness for the glory of God in the power of the Spirit.

HOWARD THURMAN ON THE HUMAN

The thought of Howard Thurman is a helpful conversation partner in this exploration of the humanizing work of the Spirit. Thurman is one of the key Black thinkers, theologians, and pastors who emphasizes "spirit" the most while also contributing insights on what it means to be a human. It is no surprise then that he is a resource, through his pastoral wisdom, for this conversation about pneumatology and race. Thurman grew up in segregated Daytona Beach, Florida, experiencing there the realities of racism. He attended Morehouse College with "Daddy" King, Martin Luther King Jr.'s father. An ordained Baptist minister, in 1953 he was named by *LIFE* magazine one of the twelve most important religious leaders in the United States. *Ebony* magazine called him one of the fifty most important figures in African American history. He advised such civil rights leaders as Martin Luther King Jr., James Farmer, and Pauli Murray, and served as dean of the chapel at Howard and Boston Universities. As one on the cutting edge of boundary-crossing ministry, he even co-founded, with a white minister, the Church for the Fellowship of All Peoples in San Francisco, California, an intentionally interracial congregation. On the basis of his life and ministry, Luther Smith calls him a "mystic prophet."[6]

5. Willie James Jennings, *Acts: A Theological Commentary on the Bible* (Louisville, KY: Westminster John Knox, 2017), 27.

6. Luther E. Smith Jr., *Howard Thurman: The Mystic as Prophet* (Richmond, IN: Friends United, 1991), 15.

But more than anything else, what is compelling about Thurman, even with all of his accolades, is that he was a genuine human being. He loved the Atlantic Ocean. He found companionship with oak trees. He learned lessons from storms at sea. He loved nature and especially penguins. He was human.[7] Before any other adjectival category was placed on him, he was human. He ministered through racism and beyond it, because of his understanding of God and God's people. His calling was to search for common ground, and that ground was our humanity. With Thurman, we see that a turn to the Spirit is a turn to the human.

We get a glimpse of Thurman's strivings and calling in the Spirit in his memorial for Dr. King at the time of King's death. He said, "[Dr. King] was killed in one sense because [hu]mankind is not quite human yet. May he live because all of us in America are closer to becoming human than ever before."[8] We are not quite human yet, but we are becoming human. This was true then, and this is still true. We are becoming human. The inhumanities and racialized violence of the past and present reveal that we are not quite human yet. But this book has attempted to nudge us in a more human and humane direction in the power of the Spirit for the life of the church.

To be human is not to escape from one's own skin or color blindness, as Thurman pondered after a seminary professor's comment,[9] nor is it erasure of racial-ethnic particularity and context. Rather, it is the recognition that we are more than any adjective, any difference, or any category. In his book *Luminous Darkness*, Thurman grapples with a definition for what it means to be a human being:

> The burden of being black and the burden of being white is [*sic*] so heavy that it is rare in our society to experience oneself as a human being. It may be, I do not know, that to experience oneself as a human being is one with experiencing one's fellows as human

---

7. Thurman scholar Walter Fluker said in an interview, "To meet Howard Thurman is to meet not a detached mystic unconcerned about the affairs of the world, but a very earthly human being." For this quote, see https://religionnews.com/2022/01/12/hartford-international-university-expands -black-ministries-with-howard-thurman-center/.

8. Howard Thurman, "Litany and Words in Memoriam: Martin Luther King, Jr.," April 7, 1968; https://www.bu.edu/htpp/files/2017/06/1968-4-07-Litany-Words-in-Memoriam-of-MLK.pdf.

9. Dr. George Cross pressed Thurman to focus on "the timeless issues of the human spirit." In response, Thurman pondered that Dr. Cross "did not know that a man and his black skin must face the 'timeless issues of the human spirit' together." See Howard Thurman, *With Head and Heart: The Autobiography of Howard Thurman* (Orlando, FL: Harvest, 1979), 60.

beings. Precisely what does it mean to experience oneself as a human being? In the first place, it means that the individual must have a sense of kinship to life that transcends and goes beyond the immediate kinship of family or the organic kinship that binds him ethnically or "racially" or nationally. He has to feel that he belongs to his total environment. He has a sense of being an essential part of the structural relationship that exists between him and all other [people], and between him, all other [people], and the total external environment. As a human being, then, he belongs to life and the whole kingdom of life that includes all that lives and perhaps, also, all that has ever lived. In other words, he sees himself as a part of a continuing, breathing, living existence. To be a human being, then, is to be essentially alive in a living world.[10]

Thurman goes further to say that "being white or black becomes merely incidental" compared to being a human being, which is more than living a racialized life. He could be charged with promoting a color-blind philosophy, which he is not, but he makes his point by giving an example of how people come together at times of disaster. In those crisis moments, people act like human beings toward each other regardless of race, class, or gender.[11] At these moments, perhaps, people ascribe to other human beings the same intrinsic worth as ascribed to the self.[12]

When Thurman was an adolescent on his way to Jacksonville, Florida, to attend a school there, he got into a bind at a Daytona Beach train station, by not having enough money to send his packed trunk to his final destination. A stranger saw him crying and eventually paid to send his trunk with him. To Thurman, this (hu)man "restored [his] broken dream"[13] and is the person to whom he dedicates his autobiography. In these situations of trouble, we are humans together, not racialized categories placed in a historical hierarchy in which the distinctions are "grounded in the necessity for exclusionary practice."[14] These distinctions operate within theological education with labels like Black, white, womanist, liberation, Latinx, and Asian. Perhaps these markings dehumanize these groups and theologies by marking them apart from what

---

10. Thurman, *Luminous Darkness*, 94.

11. Thurman, *Luminous Darkness*, 99.

12. Thurman, *Luminous Darkness*, 101.

13. See dedication page of Thurman, *With Head and Heart*.

14. Ashon Crawley, *Blackpentecostal Breath: The Aesthetics of Possibility* (New York: Fordham University Press, 2017), 15.

is normative. This is why Thurman is helpful. He moves through and reaches beyond the reality of racialization but does not "e-race" people, while gesturing toward humanization. Thus, he is a wise guide and thought partner for considering ministry with humanity in the power of the Spirit in a context of dehumanizing racialization. If "othering" others is learned by example,[15] what example can the church be and offer to unlearn othering and help humans become more humane in their interactions and relations with fellow human beings beyond the wreckage of racialization?

FOLLOW JESUS, THE HUMAN

A ministry with humanity empowered by the Spirit is deeply rooted in the humanity of Jesus, without negating the divine nature of Christ. Ministry is person-oriented, and since a turn to the Spirit turns us to Jesus, it is vital to consider how one serves (which is the meaning of "ministry") Jesus. This is distinct from speaking of "Christianity" per se, which often refers to the imperialistic, institutional structures and processes of the organization known as "the church," an entity that has been implicated in the perpetual history of racialization. To speak of Jesus, and especially the human Jesus, is not the same thing as speaking of institutional Christianity. This does not mean that the presence and power of Jesus in the Spirit cannot be found in Christianity. But the stress on Jesus the person is fundamental to a renewal of ministry that aims to humanize others in the Spirit of Jesus, because it is only through the Spirit that we can become more human like Jesus (which in turn reflects more of the divine). As Jürgen Moltmann writes, "The criterion for life in the Holy Spirit is and remains the discipleship of Jesus."[16] Those led by the Spirit follow Jesus and not necessarily the church, because at times, to follow Jesus means one has to resist the church. In his humanness, Jesus reveals the divine way of God's glory. As the Spirit shapes us to become more humane, she forms us to become more human, like Jesus.

Especially for those who have historically been racialized, rather than humanized, Thurman's overall intellectual and pastoral project

15. Toni Morrison, *The Origin of Others* (Cambridge, MA: Harvard University Press, 2017), 6.

16. Jürgen Moltmann, *The Source of Life: The Holy Spirit and the Theology of Life* (Minneapolis: Fortress, 1997), 62.

is one of reclaiming Black humanity for all humanity. He begins his classic book *Jesus and the Disinherited* with a chapter on the human Jesus. He does not deny the metaphysical interpretations of Jesus, but his emphasis is on those who are suffering, oppressed, and disinherited. For this reason he begins with Jesus, the earthly human one. Jesus was a Jew of Palestine. Jesus was also poor. Jesus was born into poverty; thus he was the Son of Man (or as the Common English Bible translates it, "the Human One"), in solidarity with the masses of poor people around the world. Jesus was also a part of a minoritized group under the Roman Empire. He was a brown-skinned brother from Bethlehem. This situates Jesus within the human condition, not his divine power, amid an imperial system of domination and death, suggesting that a Christian ministry with humanity necessarily takes the humanity of Jesus seriously.

In the incarnation, God the Son became human, a holy gesture that signaled the embrace of all of humanity. Likewise, God the Spirit ministers to and loves the world in human ways. To touch us, heal us, and save us, God worked through human flesh. As John writes, "The Word became flesh and lived among us" (John 1:14). The divine Word became human, living, breathing as a human being, the "divine housed in a body like ours."[17] As Barbara Brown Taylor writes, "God trusted flesh and blood to bring divine love to earth."[18] Ministry is a human flesh-and-blood calling, rooted in Jesus Christ, the Human One, whose life is "the paradigm of humanization."[19]

But as noted already, the particular human form that Jesus takes is distinct and illuminating for this conversation on race. According to the Christ hymn in Philippians 2, "Christ Jesus, . . . though he was in the form of God, did not regard equality with God as something to be exploited, but emptied himself, taking the form of a slave, being born in human likeness. And being found in human form, he humbled himself and became obedient to the point of death—even death on a cross" (Phil. 2:5–8). God in Christ took on a human form, more specifically the form of a slave. What happens to this Christ-slave is what occurs to many enslaved people throughout history: they are killed, crucified. The human form of Jesus is cruciform; that matters for ministry to

17. Anthony B. Pinn, *Embodiment and the New Shape of Black Theological Thought* (New York: New York University Press, 2010), 97.

18. Barbara Brown Taylor, *An Altar in the World: A Geography of Faith* (New York: HarperCollins, 2009), 48.

19. Kim, *Preaching in an Age of Globalization*, 53.

those who have been racialized and dehumanized in the world. It matters that God took on the human flesh of a slave. In the incarnation, we see that God takes on the kind of life so often threatened by death, in order to save the world from death. But this particular human form also points to another key aspect of doing ministry with humanity.

ATTEND TO SUFFERING BODIES

The human form of Jesus challenges a ministry with humanity to be attentive to suffering bodies, particularly marginalized ones. It is vital to affirm that "the incarnation of Jesus is proof of the importance of the body as a means of grace."[20] The body is a subject of ministry and an object to receive ministry. Humans are enfleshed creatures whose bodies are temples of the Spirit. Ministry includes words but also actions, enfleshed speech, lived sermons. Augustine believed that one's life could be an eloquent speech.[21] Ministry requires our whole selves, whole lives, not just our minds, but all of our bodies, whatever color, shape, or ability. How could it be any other way when we serve a God who became a body in Jesus?

It is clear that when God comes, "God comes, aiming for ecstasy in the body of the creature."[22] The body is a site of practical theological knowledge. The body knows, goes, flows in the Spirit to do ministry. It is an epistemological source and resource for the practice of ministry and reveals that through the incarnation words matter, but they are to be incarnate words. A ministry with humanity reminds us that human beings are more than a head on a pile of books. To proclaim the gospel in word and deed necessitates a whole human person, spiritual and physical, the spirit and the body, the spirit in the body and the body in the spirit. Only a whole person can do holy ministry wholly. Lee Butler writes,

> Is the spirit willing and the flesh weak? I do not think that is the lesson we learn from the passion of the Christ child. The message that comes to us from the empty tomb is the spirit is willing and

20. N. Lynne Westfield, *Dear Sisters: A Womanist Practice of Hospitality* (Cleveland: Pilgrim, 2007), 86.

21. Augustine, *On Christian Doctrine*, Book IV; accessed January 7, 2022, https://faculty.georgetown.edu/jod/augustine/ddc4.html.

22. Willie James Jennings, *After Whiteness: An Education in Belonging* (Grand Rapids: Eerdmans, 2020), 143.

the flesh is too! Without embodiment, why should we have hope in the rapture or dream of walking around Heaven? If the spirit is willing the flesh must be equally willing. What does it mean to be a "living soul" if not the integration of spirit and body? Maintaining a hierarchal split between spirit and body diminishes our humanity and denies the gospel of the abundant life.[23]

In the Spirit, ministers take the human body seriously as a vessel of grace and goodness to be embraced as vital for doing genuinely human ministry.

Furthermore, in light of the particular body of Jesus, and its cruciform character as a slave, attention should also be given to the wounded nature of human existence. This is particularly critical in light of the history and reality of racialization. At the heart of Christian faith and ministry stands the wounded, suffering human body of Jesus. As the hymn writers put it: Jesus was "wounded for me."[24] A Christian reading of the Servant Song of Isaiah would interpret these words to reflect Jesus: "he was wounded for our transgressions, crushed for our iniquities" (Isa. 53:5). The material body of Christ is wounded and scarred. It is a blues body. James Cone calls it a "lynched black body,"[25] a tortured body hanging from a tree calling us to the suffering ones of the world, crying out to us to see the marginalized mangled because of the mess of sin. "Were you there when they crucified my Lord?" the spiritual asks. This theological memory interweaves the cultural memory of broken Black and othered bodies with the tortured and broken body of Jesus. Culturally and theologically, there is a wound. For African Americans, as Joanne Terrell puts it, "Jesus' death by crucifixion is a prototype of African Americans' death by circumscription"[26] and reveals his identification with and compassion for the oppressed and dehumanized. Jesus is not a well-manicured, pedicured, nip and tuck, Clorox-bleached, Botox, cosmetic, plastic-surgery-seeking Christ. He is fully human and his wounds from the crucifixion were not erased by the resurrection.

23. Lee Butler, "The Spirit Is Willing and the Flesh Is Too: Living Whole and Holy Lives through Integrating Spirituality and Sexuality," in *Loving the Body: Black Religious Studies and the Erotic*, ed. Anthony B. Pinn and Dwight N. Hopkins (New York: Palgrave Macmillan, 2004), 120.

24. W. G. Ovens and Gladys Westcott Roberts, "Wounded for Me," *The New National Baptist Hymnal*, 21st-Century Edition (Nashville: Triad, 2001), 111.

25. James Cone, "Strange Fruit: The Cross and the Lynching Tree," *The African American Pulpit* 11, no. 2 (Spring 2008): 24.

This human, brutalized, disinherited Jesus beckons us from a lynching tree, not only to recall the cross of Calvary, but to remember that he
had no place to lay his head and existed on the borderlands of humanity,
along with those who were hungry, thirsty, naked, in prison, enslaved,
unemployed, without health care, and in public schools with inadequate resources. This attunement to human suffering in all its manifestations is an attunement to a human God who had a particular mission
from the position of a slave. This human form informed what Jesus did
in ministry. Willie Jennings writes, "Rooted in the slave's position aims
at a much more intense public reality—that of addressing the powers
that enslave people economically, politically, socially, spiritually, and
physically."[27] That God's body became a slave's body in Christ matters
for how we teach, preach, think, serve, and live out the Christian faith
in the face of a racialized reality.

What Jesus did was an extension of who he was. Unsurprisingly, the
focus of his anointed ministry, which should also be the focus of ours,
was on broken lives, broken bodies, and a broken society—what could
be called a wounded world. In what some call his inaugural sermon,
in Luke 4, Jesus makes it plain: "The Spirit of the Lord is upon me,
because he has anointed me to bring good news to the poor. He has
sent me to proclaim release to the captives and recovery of sight to the
blind, to let the oppressed go free, to proclaim the year of the Lord's
favor" (Luke 4:18–19). Jesus makes it clear that his gospel, his mission,
his life's work, centers on the marginalized—those who are poor, captives, blind, and oppressed.

This is the heart of a ministry with humanity, one that seeks to humanize the dehumanized, one that is not race-based but human-centered.
The focus of Christ's ministry is on those who have been downtrodden
by the politically powerful and privileged, those who have been dehumanized and ostracized because of racialization. He spoke and lived a
political gospel, shaking up a status quo society. He was the embodiment of the "Spirit of God—Without-Within"[28] who blew inwardly
and outwardly and worked for personal and social transformation, for

26. JoAnne Marie Terrell, *Power in the Blood? The Cross in the African American Experience* (Maryknoll, NY: Orbis, 1998), 34.

27. Willie James Jennings, "Speaking Gospel in the Public Arena," in *Preaching Gospel: Essays in
Honor of Richard Lischer*, ed. Charles L. Campbell, Clayton J. Schmit, Mary Hinkle Shore, Jennifer E.
Copeland (Eugene, OR: Cascade, 2016), 187–97.

28. Howard Thurman, *The Centering Moment* (New York: Harper & Bros., 1969), 21.

29. Howard Thurman, *Jesus and the Disinherited* (repr., Boston: Beacon, 1996), 11.

the liberation of the oppressed. None of this should be surprising, in that Jesus was a poor, oppressed Jew, a member of the disinherited class himself. Like him, his gospel was centered on the weak and those "with their backs against the wall."[29]

The Spirit is sensitive to those suffering and attuned to the daily struggles of all human beings and works to free those who are enslaved. Like the poem of Emma Lazarus, "The New Colossus," Jesus might say:

> Give me your tired, your poor,
> Your huddled masses yearning to breathe free,
> The wretched refuse of your teeming shore.
> Send these, the homeless, tempest-tost to me.[30]

Give me those who cannot breathe. Give me those who were shot in the back just because they were Black. Give me those who are tossed away like trash or treated like dung. A ministry with humanity in the Spirit of Jesus proclaims, "Give me those who have been dehumanized because they have been racialized."

In the classic TV series *M*A*S*H*, set in a mobile army hospital during the Korean War, doctors received a patient who believed he was Jesus Christ. Arnold Chandler had been a bombardier in an airplane and had dropped many bombs on other human beings. Because of the trauma of it all, one day his mind snapped, and he decided that he was no longer a man named Arnold Chandler. He was Christ the Lord. This appeared to be a mental condition that would require a lot of therapy. A psychiatrist eventually came to the man and said, "You say you are Christ, and yet here you are in an army hospital in the middle of a war. What would Jesus be doing here?" With tears streaming down his face, this supposedly mentally ill man replied with these words: "I am Christ the Lord, where else should I be? These are my children."[31]

That tear-stained Jesus would be among ailing and hurting humans in the middle of a war should not surprise us. By coming in the form of a slave he entered the ongoing human struggle in the world. To have a ministry with humanity calls us to be proximate to pain, regardless of race or life situation. Pain, struggle, and woundedness cannot be avoided. It is the broader context for ministry as a whole. Even for the

30. Emma Lazarus, "The New Colossus," accessed January 7, 2022, https://www.poetryfoundation.org/poems/46550/the-new-colossus.

31. This story is told in Scott Hoezee, *Actuality: Real Life Stories for Sermons That Matter* (Nashville: Abingdon, 2014), 113.

topic of race and racism, "as people of faith, we are all called to attend to the suffering of one another. In order to attend to this suffering, we need to first acknowledge that it exists. Racism continues to exist and refusing to name it will not make it go away."[32] Racialization will not go away in this world, yet this does not mean that we should not strive in the Spirit toward a ministry with humanity. What is critical in this endeavor, in light of the Spirit of Jesus, is for ministry with humanity to make "an oath of allegiance with those who suffer,"[33] those with afflicted bodies, racialized bodies, bruised bodies, neglected bodies, and forgotten bodies. By doing so, one will realize the breadth of crucified humanity in the world such that we acknowledge to each other, "I Need You to Survive."[34]

STRIVE FOR COMMUNITY

These suffering, battered human bodies are not merely individualized flesh but are actually "spirited bodies in relationship."[35] This points to a broader community, a collective body that is also often hurting. What this means, therefore, is that ministry with humanity is done in community for the community and always strives for deeper relations. Rather than accentuate differences, no matter how beautiful, ministry in this way centers on what is common between people, and this "common is created by the Spirit."[36] In the overflow of the Pentecost experience in Acts, after Peter's sermon and a baptism, we learn that "all who believed were together and had all things in common; they would sell their possessions and goods and distribute the proceeds to all, as any had need. Day by day, as they spent much time together in the temple, they broke bread at home and ate their food with glad and generous hearts, praising God and having the goodwill of all the people" (Acts 2:44–47). There was the sharing of resources, sharing of place, sharing worship, sharing food, and an overall sharing of life together as they

---

32. Carolyn Helsel, *Preaching about Racism: A Guide for Faith Leaders* (St. Louis: Chalice, 2018), 4.

33. Claudio Carvalhaes, *What's Worship Got to Do with It? Interpreting Life Liturgically* (Eugene, OR: Cascade, 2018), 7.

34. This is a gospel song by Hezekiah Walker, "I Need You to Survive," track 7 on *The Essential Hezekiah Walker*, Zomba Recording LLC, 1992.

35. Johnny Ramírez-Johnson, "Intercultural Communication Skills for a Missiology of Interdependent Mutuality," in *Can "White" People Be Saved?: Triangulating Race, Theology, and Mission*, ed. Love L. Sechrest, Johnny Ramírez-Johnson, and Amos Yong (Downers Grove, IL: InterVarsity, 2018), 260.

36. Jennings, *Acts*, 39.

looked out for each other's needs. It was a crossing of the borders, out of selfish enclaves to a fuller, new life in the Spirit. During the times of segregation in the United States, the breaking of bread together by different racialized groups constituted a kind of "lung"[37] where the breath of the Spirit could breathe. It was a common breath, a ministry for the entire community in need, regardless of linguistic, ethnic, or economic variation.

To have all things in common is truly aspirational and pneumatological, a desire and work of the Spirit. So often it is the racialized distinction that creates walls between humanity rather than the hoped-for "joining"[38] and new realities of relationships through which we "gesture communion with our very existence."[39] It is too easy to close the doors of our hearts and resources to others, especially the racially different, rather than fling wide the doors of our lives. A ministry with humanity aims to bring people together in a communal Spirit, in the same way the spirituals of enslaved Blacks functioned.[40] The spirituals belong to the community, as seen in their lack of designated individual authors or composers. There is no hierarchy embedded in them and through them, which is why these songs of the Spirit have transgressed racial, ethnic, linguistic, geographical, and economic boundaries for centuries, as they are sung all over the world. These songs reveal how the Spirit moves through and beyond the social construction of race to the diverse reflections of the human across the earth. They rose out of a particular historical, cultural context and from the racialized Black flesh and voices of the enslaved. Yet under the aegis of the Spirit, they are human songs, not just Black songs, which is why they are found in the tongues and bodies of all flesh. Through the Spirit(ual), humans are drawn together to share in life.

The Spirit opens us up to one another, and ministry with humanity strives for this opening, this new humanity in Christ (Eph. 2:15) or "cosmopolitan citizenship."[41] As Christians, we aim not for "gated

---

37. Howard Thurman, "Black Pentecost #1: The Release of the Spirit," delivered during the Black Ecumenical Commission of Massachusetts meeting at Eliot Congregational Church, Roxbury, MA, May 30, 1972; http://archives.bu.edu/web/howard-thurman/virtual-listening-room/detail?id=360482.

38. Willie James Jennings, *The Christian Imagination: Theology and the Origins of Race* (New Haven, CT: Yale University Press, 2010), 267.

39. Jennings, *After Whiteness*, 152.

40. Eunjoo Kim presents a theology of humanization, and one aspect of it is a communal process rooted in the social doctrine of the Trinity. See Kim, *Preaching in an Age of Globalization*, 43–64.

41. Jennings, *Christian Imagination*, 10.

enclaves" of racialization but for a "gospel of human race equality," rooted in the breath of the Spirit.[42] Without erasing the beauty of particularity, the Spirit crowns our mutual humanity, our relational call-and-response, in beloved harmony.

When Baby Suggs, holy, preached in the Clearing, it was the literal and figurative harmony of the community that completed the sermon. Toni Morrison writes that when she spoke with her twisted hip what was on her heart, "others opened their mouths and gave her the music. Long notes held until the four-part harmony was perfect enough for their deeply loved flesh."[43] The collective body harmonized as a means of healing humanization in the midst of their brokenness due to racialization and slavery. The collective suffering body finished the sermon. Their harmony was a re-sounding way to beat back the powers that attempted to destroy them. This sermon is deeply communal, where no human member is left out. Every-body is incorporated as the Spirit is poured out on all flesh, all beaten bodies. The four-part harmony represents more than music: a harmonious community that is the goal of ministry with humanity in the Spirit.

As Dr. King put it: "We are caught in an inescapable network of mutuality tied in a single garment of destiny."[44] In a 1963 sermon at Marsh Chapel, Boston University, Howard Thurman preached that there was a "profound ground of unity" between human beings and encouraged listeners: "Keep open the doors of thy heart. It matters not how many doors close against thee."[45] Ministry entails human vulnerability and openness to the other, even if the other may do you harm. Further, Thurman says that "the thing that human beings need in order to realize themselves, in order that that which is potential in them might be actualized, is other human beings. We must have each other. . . . We come to ourselves in the human encounter."[46] "We belong to each other, we belong together."[47] With this understanding,

42. James A. Forbes Jr., *Whose Gospel? A Concise Guide to Progressive Protestantism* (New York: The New Press, 2010), 86.

43. Toni Morrison, *Beloved* (1987; New York: Vintage, 2004), 104.

44. Martin Luther King Jr., "Letter from a Birmingham Jail," Martin Luther King, Jr. Research and Education Institute, 1963, accessed January 7, 2022, http://okra.stanford.edu/transcription/document _images/undecided/630416-019.pdf.

45. Howard Thurman, "The Wider Ministry and The Concept of Community," delivered at Marsh Chapel in Boston, MA, July 28, 1963; accessed January 7, 2022, https://www.bu.edu/htpp/files /2017/10/Wider-Ministry-and-the-Concept-of-Community-July-28-1963.pdf.

46. Thurman, "The Wider Ministry," 2.

47. Jennings, *After Whiteness*, 10.

community is the goal, "whole-making" is the goal.[48] To be whole means to be in community with others, with those who are different and have been ostracized. If a person isolates themselves, they diminish themselves. If a person shuts another person away, that is their own destruction.[49] To do ministry with humanity involves seeking to nourish each other beyond the racialized walls that divide and block mutuality and genuine love. By engaging with the other, our "little [lives]" become "larger."[50] Without each other in community, we become smaller and less human, because we were created to be in relationship as a reflection of the image of God, just as in Genesis when male and female together illuminate God's image (Gen. 1:27).

This is because the Spirit nudges us toward communion with God and each other across all of the divides of racialized difference. "There is a spirit abroad in life . . . a spirit that makes for wholeness and for community."[51] A ministry with humanity aims for wholeness; that can happen only if we recognize our human need for each other and that we belong to each other because we belong to God, God's body, broken. Yet even in our brokenness as splintered people, we can experience a sense of gratitude for life and for each other's lives, knowing that we were made for togetherness. When we are not together, we are less human, for our full humanity flourishes in human community.[52] As Frantz Fanon wrote, "[The Black man and the white man] have to move away from the inhuman voices of their respective ancestors so that a genuine communication can be born,"[53] a genuine chance for cherished communion. Ministry in the Spirit aims for humanness and common life and is wise enough to know that those things we might use to protect ourselves from one another can become our own "executioner."[54] Thus, rather than fight with and divide each other to destroy community, the human way is to embrace the wonder of our common finitude, our mortality.

48. Howard Thurman, *The Search for Common Ground* (Richmond, IN: Friends United, 1986), 76.

49. Thurman, *Search for Common Ground*, 104.

50. Thurman, *Luminous Darkness*, 95.

51. Thurman, *Luminous Darkness*, 112.

52. Carolyn Helsel provides a unique perspective on gratitude in relation to dealing with preaching and racism. See Helsel, *Preaching about Racism*, 11–14. She presents a positive approach to combating racialization by placing gratitude into this conversation. Her distinct view reminds us that our thanksgiving, our Eucharist, is rooted in a crucified man. There can be gratitude and grace in the face of racism.

53. Frantz Fanon, *Black Skin, White Masks* (New York: Grove, 1952), 206.

54. Thurman, *Jesus and the Disinherited*, 46.

EMBRACE MORTALITY

Too often, the church defines theology and ministry primarily in terms of morality and the "culture war." But ministry with humanity in the power of the Spirit stresses our shared mortality, rather than a feigned morality. God's designation for the prophet Ezekiel applies to all of us: we are mortals (Ezek. 37:3, 9, 11, 15). We are God's mortals, God's children, God's creation. As God's, "our worth is the gracious gift of divine love."[55] Because of this love, all human beings are valuable and equal. Black humanity and all humanity are loved and affirmed by God. This is fundamental for adhering to "reverence for personality."[56] We revere one another because of our common humanity, the imprint of God's Spirit in our lives, in our hearts, and on our flesh.

Even though racialized conversations and tactics seek to divide, in the Spirit we are propelled to have "all things in common," and that common ground is that all human beings are from the ground. "We are joined at the site of the dirt, and the dirt is our undeniable kin. Even geographic distance and the difference of strange tongues cannot thwart this truth—we are creatures bound together."[57] Humans are bound in and to the ground, which is where we discover the kinship of humanity, not separated social races. A ministry with humanity embraces humanness and commonness between all people and works for the common good rooted in the common ground of God.

Constructive theology, particularly pneumatology, engages the ground, the land, the dirt and dust of God. Only through the reception of the gift of the Spirit will human beings touch each other in the common earth. Good news is discovered there in the soil as well, the good news that we are human beings created in the image of God, formed from the dust of the earth, the good news that the imprimatur of the Creator is on all flesh and not just on one race. In the dirt or dust of God, there is no human hierarchy, because we are all grounded in

---

55. Forbes, *Whose Gospel?*, 84–85.

56. Thurman, *Jesus and the Disinherited*, 106. A dominant biblical theme in Black preaching praxis is creation and the idea of the personhood of Blacks rooted in God's creation of all humanity, thus *imago Dei*. See Dale Andrews, "Black Preaching Praxis," in *Black Church Studies: An Introduction*, ed. Carol B. Duncan, Juan Marcial Floyd-Thomas, and Stacey M. Floyd-Thomas (Nashville: Abingdon, 2007), 215.

57. Willie James Jennings, "Can White People Be Saved? Reflections on the Relationship of Missions and Whiteness," in *Can "White" People Be Saved?: Triangulating Race, Theology, and Mission*, ed. Love L. Sechrest, Johnny Ramírez-Johnson, and Amos Yong (Downers Grove, IL: InterVarsity, 2018), 30.

God. "To embrace one's humanity [in this way] is not mere humanism but good theology."[58]

A ministry empowered by the Spirit recognizes that although there have been "different Christianities,"[59] there is one humanity, one race, the human race. After whiteness, there is humanness, a way through and beyond racialized concepts of whiteness or blackness or distinct otherness. In the Spirit, ministry is not about race in its social or even faulty biological framework; it is about being human and becoming more fully human, even as the community writ large is made up of different socialized races. To constantly talk about or emphasize "race" only reifies this colonial social construction of dehumanization.

This project has aimed to "de-fang"[60] colonial racism in the power of the Spirit by gesturing toward a new tongue, language, and way of speaking about and dealing with racialized issues in the church in particular. As noted, the common denominator for us is that we all have come from God and to God we all will return. All humans are "spawned from the womb of the earth,"[61] which indicates that we are all *humus*, meaning "from the earth." All humans, regardless of race or ethnicity, are from the earth, are from dust, are dust. We are from dust and to dust we will return (Gen. 3:19). We do not need Ash Wednesday to tell us this. We should know this when helicopters crash, when cancer takes another life, when mysterious viruses take root across the globe. Human life, human beings, are fragile, are dust blown around the earth's surface. But this is the common ground, the soil of the Spirit we have been searching for—the ground of the earth. Feet on the ground. Bodies from the ground and to the ground. Dust and ashes. Human, from the earth. If a ministry with humanity would nurture what I call an "ethics of dust," in which we remember that we are all dust and will return to dust, this might shape our interactions with one another across the racial chasms, and then perhaps we might actually find the time, place, and heart for a joyous communion with brothers and sisters of all races, tongues, nations, and tribes.

This type of ministry with humanity demonstrates how the Spirit moves preaching and other forms of ministry beyond rhetoric to an

58. Richard Lischer, *The End of Words: The Language of Reconciliation in a Culture of Violence* (Grand Rapids: Eerdmans, 2005), 136.

59. Jennings, *Christian Imagination*, 4.

60. Morrison, *Origin of Others*, 53.

61. Thurman, *Search for Common Ground*, xvi.

ethic, to enfleshed human forms and practices.[62] The Spirit shapes and empowers this ethic to seek human wholeness as individuals, as communities, and in relation to God. This ethic of and in the humanizing Spirit can be viewed as part of the sanctification process, a sanctification conceived as "Spiritification." This ethic is a way of life in the Spirit and means that the Spirit is always pressing us beyond any one practice toward people, human beings, loving humans, serving humans, with the recognition that we are more alike than different.

We have a *humus* home of dust and are mortal. Remembering that we are dust might help us discover new directions that the Spirit might be moving in relation to conversations about and practices around race in the church. Perhaps dust and breath, soil and Spirit, will propel us to have a human conversation in the church because the Holy Spirit humanizes rather than dehumanizes. One might even say that the Spirit rehumanizes us as she reminds us how to be human together, embodying the revivification of humanization, a rehumanization in the face of dehumanization.

A FINAL CALL TO TOGETHERNESS

A turn to the Spirit is a turn to the human, not a racialized being. There are some who want to close the distance between us, earthly creatures, who are on the earth and from the earth. Toni Morrison asks, "Why should we want to close the distance when we can close the gate?"[63] Why? Because we are already close, as close as the dirt and dust of our common home as mortals, as close as the common breath in our bodies from the Spirit. Archbishop Desmond Tutu would answer that question, "[Because] we were made for togetherness." If we try to be self-sufficient, we are "subhuman."[64] In other words, to be human is to be together in the communion of the Spirit. On the day of Pentecost, they were "all together" in their diversity of humanity, and something powerful blew their way and through their lives for the life of the world, confirming the saying, "If you want to go fast, go alone; if you want to go far, go together."

---

62. For perspectives on what this ethic might include, see *The Holy Spirit and Social Justice: Interdisciplinary Global Perspectives,* ed. Antipas L. Harris and Michael D. Palmer (Lanham, MD: Seymour, 2019).

63. Morrison, *Origin of Others,* 38.

64. Desmond Tutu, *In God's Hands* (New York: Bloomsbury, 2014), 34.

Tim Hansel tells a story about Jimmy Durante, one of the great entertainers of the twentieth century:

> He was asked to be a part of a show for World War II veterans. He told them his schedule was very busy so he could afford only a few minutes and do one short monologue and then immediately leave for his next appointment. The show's director agreed and was happy that he was coming even with his busy schedule. When Jimmy got on stage, something interesting happened. He performed his short monologue but then he stayed. The applause grew louder and louder and he kept staying. Fifteen, twenty, then thirty minutes went by. Finally, he took his last bow and left the stage. Someone backstage stopped him and said, "I thought you had to go after a few minutes. What happened?" Jimmy answered, "I did have to go, but I can show you the reason I stayed. You can see for yourself if you'll look down on the front row." He pointed to the front row and in the front row were two men, each of whom had lost an arm in the war. One had lost his right arm and the other had lost his left. But together, they were able to clap, and that's exactly what they were doing, loudly and cheerfully.[65]

Left hand and right hand, together. Together, they did not focus on what they lost but focused on what they had in community. This is why one could hear during slavery the words of this spiritual: "Walk together children and don't get weary." Together, we will be able to do a reconciling work that we could never do apart. Left and right, together. Liberal and conservative, together. Black and white, together. This search and hope for common ground in the Spirit and a robust mortal ministry with humanity are rooted in a God who has a conjunctive imagination. "From every nation, from all tribes and peoples and languages" (Rev. 7:9), together. "Parthians, Medes, Elamites, and residents of Mesopotamia, Judea and Cappadocia, Pontus and Asia, Phrygia and Pamphylia, Egypt and the parts of Libya belonging to Cyrene, and visitors from Rome, both Jews and proselytes, Cretans and Arabs" (Acts 2:9–11), together. Baptists and Episcopalians, Presbyterians and Lutherans, Methodists and Catholics and Nazarenes, Church of God (Anderson) and Church of God (Cleveland) and Church of God in Christ, holy rollers and the frozen chosen, from east and west, north and south, meeting for fellowship at the wedding supper of the Lamb

---

65. Tim Hansel, *Holy Sweat* (Nashville: W Publishing Group, 1987), 104–5.

of God, Jesus Christ, drinking wine and eating bread. God functions with conjunctions and possesses a conjunctive imagination, not a disjunctive one. God's intention is for the church to be made up of people from every nation, language, gender, race, class, ethnicity, political persuasion, family history and educational background. All flesh can receive the Spirit to become the world house of God, together. With this understanding for Christian ministry and life, no human being exists outside of God's love, because God is not a racist.

When it comes to the history of racialized inhumanities, God, Jesus, and the Spirit are not the problem; *we* are. When Howard Thurman asked Gandhi, "What is the greatest handicap that Jesus has in India?" Gandhi replied, "Christianity."[66] My hope is that through this exploratory wrestling of the interface of pneumatology and race for the life of the church, readers will walk away with a blessing, filled with honesty, humanity, and hope, because the winds of the Spirit are still blowing new possibilities into the world, in order for us to embody the conjunctive imagination of God in the Spirit of Jesus.

In this Spirit, may we commit our flesh to this common and holy calling, this common ground, human to human, earth to earth, ashes to ashes, dust to dust. As we do so, may we remember these words of Thurman:

> It is the intent of life, that we, that we shall all be one people. For better or for worse we are tied together in one bundle and I can never be what I must be until you are what you must be: for better or for worse this is the only option. And to reject it is to reject life. And to reject life is . . . to make God repent that he ever gave us a chance to live.[67]

66. Thurman, *Luminous Darkness*, 104.

67. Howard Thurman, "Litany and Words in Memoriam: Martin Luther King, Jr.," April 7, 1968, https://www.bu.edu/htpp/files/2017/06/1968-4-07-Litany-Words-in-Memoriam-of-MLK.pdf.

Deep River:
A Coda on Humility, Mystery,
and the Holy Spirit

An aspect of our humanness, our *humus*-ness, is humility. When it comes to the Holy Spirit in general and this conversation about race and the church in particular, a level of intellectual and spiritual humility is required. To be human is to be humble, even though this may not always be obvious in our daily lives. This exploration of the fruit of pneumatology for engaging race and racism has been only a glimpse of what might be possible in the Spirit to move us through and beyond racialization to a more human way of being and living, because we see only "through a glass darkly" (1 Cor. 13:12 KJV). As a finite human being, I am limited in my knowledge about the Holy Spirit and race, but this does not prevent my attempt to be constructive to assist the church to move forward in helpful and holy ways.

Yet it is important to remember, "The Spirit of God can never be reduced to a projection of human experience—whether personal or corporate."[1] Human beings are not the same as the Holy Spirit, just as our theologies of God are not synonymous with the reality of God. Humility can be an indication that we understand that the Spirit is a revealed and concealed mystery, and thus that we will not know everything there is to know about God or even the topic of race and how

1. William C. Turner, "Pneumatology: Contributions from African American Christian Thought to the Pentecostal Theological Task," in *Afro-Pentecostalism: Black Pentecostal and Charismatic Christianity in History and Culture*, ed. Amos Yong and Estrelda Y. Alexander (New York: New York University Press, 2011), 182.

it has shaped the entire world.[2] How can one fully know about divine breath or wind when it is free and uncontrollable?[3]

Take, for example, a story in Acts. In that story, some disciples from Ephesus came to the apostle Paul and said, "We have not even heard that there is a Holy Spirit" (Acts 19:2). These believers, these disciples, did not know everything or hear everything that there was to hear about God, the church, and faith. They still had much to learn on the highway to spiritual growth. They knew or understood some things but not everything about God's way. Being disciples called for some humility as they sought to follow the way of Jesus more faithfully and receive the Holy Spirit into their lives. They were fine with not knowing everything there was to know, because they were humble enough to know that they did not have to have all the answers to follow Jesus in the Spirit. What happened next revealed what life in the Spirit truly was and is.

When Paul heard that they had not received the Holy Spirit, he laid hands on them to receive the Spirit. When he did, the Spirit came upon them, and they spoke in tongues and prophesied, that is, they received the gift of both unintelligibility (tongues) and intelligibility (prophesying). They understood what was said, and they did not understand what was spoken; both comprehension and incomprehension are gifts of the Spirit, because the Spirit is as mysterious as the wind. *Not knowing or understanding is a gift of the Spirit, along with knowing.* There are some things in life we just cannot explain, because we cannot exhaust an inexhaustible God. In the Spirit, we come to know how much we do not know as Christians, which means we do not have to have all the answers to the issue of race, racism, and the church. This does not mean we do not strive to do better and be better and become more fully human and Christlike. It means we recognize that we have limits as finite creatures because we are not an infinite God. What has been explored in this book is provisional and by no means exhaustive in terms of all that can be said. It has been a humble attempt to aid the church to become more like Jesus in word and deed as it relates to race and racism.

2. For more about the function of cultural humility in race relations, see this essay by Ishmael Ruiz-Millan, "Cultural Humility Can Help Us Become Better Leaders and Better Christians," *Faith & Leadership*, February 5, 2019, https://faithandleadership.com/ismael-ruiz-millan-cultural-humility -can-help-us-become-better-leaders-and-better-christians.

3. For more about the Spirit and mystery, see Steven R. Guthrie, *Creator Spirit: The Holy Spirit and the Art of Becoming Human* (Grand Rapids: Baker Academic, 2011), 1–21.

Even the prophet Ezekiel, in the context of the Spirit leading him to a valley of dry bones, comes to learn about incomprehensibility or unknowability in the life of faith. God asks Ezekiel, "Mortal, can these bones live?" [and Ezekiel] answers, "O Lord GOD, you know" (Ezek. 37:3). Ezekiel acknowledges that he does not know the answer to God's question about the bones living again. He is humble and honest and claims his incomprehension and says, "O Lord GOD, you know." This theology and spirituality of incomprehensibility is a true path in wrestling with a raced world and church. We know and we do not know how best to proceed in words and actions. But although we embrace the mystery of the Holy Spirit as a part of an anointed life and ministry,[4] we continue to work toward the loving communion and eternal conjunction of God for all people, regardless of race, ethnicity, language, class, or gender.

Can we move beyond and through racialization to humanization, in the power of the Spirit? Can these bones live, once and for all? In the Spirit, our answer should always be: "O Lord God, you know."

---

4. James Forbes writes, "Acknowledging that we know not is one step toward achieving an anointed ministry." See his *The Holy Spirit and Preaching* (Nashville: Abingdon, 1989), 61.

Index

CPSIA information can be obtained
at www.ICGtesting.com
Printed in the USA
LVHW112237141022
730587LV00003B/6

9 780664 267223